SUPERCHARGED FOOD

EAT RIGHT

FOR YOUR SHAPE

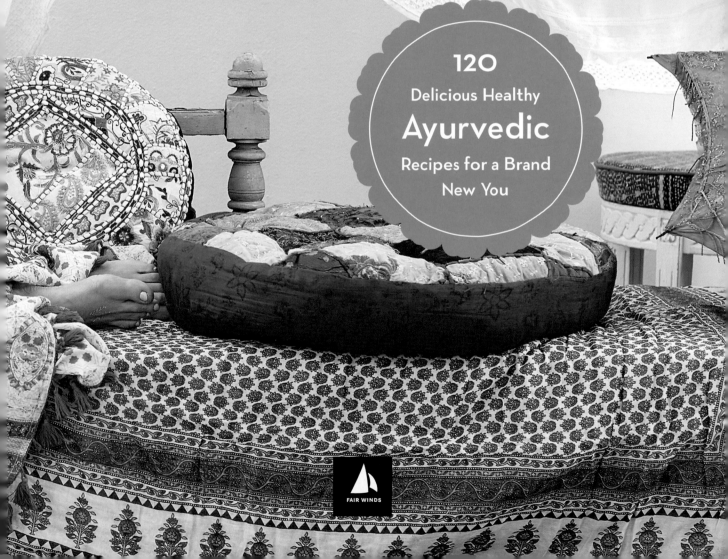

SUPERCHARGED FOOD

EAT RIGHT
FOR YOUR SHAPE

Lee Holmes

120
Delicious Healthy
Ayurvedic
Recipes for a Brand
New You

FAIR WINDS

Contents

Introduction

I could use this introduction just to talk about me, but "about me" pages can sometimes be overly self-aware. I don't want to impose on you a list of achievements and have you yawning mid-sentence the first time you pick this book up. So while I'm keen to jazz up my introduction with a bit of background, I want to make this book all about *you* – the person I wrote it for.

To begin with, though, I'd like to invite you to discover a little bit more about me so that you'll be able to get the most out of this book, which has been cooked up in the Ayurvedic kitchens of India during my travels there. I want you to be able to use this book in your own kitchen and feel excited about the recipes, enjoying their special and unique feel-good curative capabilities. I'd be particularly honored if you used this book regularly and were inspired to share the recipes with your family and friends.

I believe that this is more than just a book about losing weight and eating right for your shape. It's a book you can turn to at any point in your life to get in touch with your constitutional needs and understand how to bring harmony into your life through food, nutrition, mindfulness and meditation.

If I were to describe myself in three phrases, I would probably say I was sometimes introspective and a little bit funny, with an overdose of creativity. This is my fifth book and I've really enjoyed seeing the writing appear almost like magic on the blank pages. I want you to know that I'm not just talking the talk here, and I hope that once you've immersed yourself in the pages, my authenticity will shine through. I've been walking the Ayurvedic walk ever since I incorporated and implemented its principles into my life after taking a trip to India to study Ayurvedic cookery and nutrition first hand, and I'm eager to share my game-changing results with you.

When I commenced the Ayurvedic lifestyle, I was a healthy size 12 and had just treated my fibromyalgia and an autoimmune problem through eating anti-inflammatory foods. Since adopting this new way of life, I'm feeling the best I have ever felt and am now a healthy size 10. Whatever size you are or desire to be, the recipes and principles in this book will help you to bring your body into balance so that you'll become the size and shape you were always meant to be.

The ingredients used in this book come directly from nature, and I've included nutritionally dense foods with potent healing properties so that you can enjoy food the healthy way. One of the big attractions of the recipes is that they're created with simple ingredients that are grown and picked in tune with the seasons, which makes them so full of flavor and undeniably satisfying. A home truth about Ayurveda is its emphasis on freshly prepared earth-based foods.

I hope you enjoy delving into the richness and healing properties of Ayurvedic nutrition and

Meeting Tony the local grocer and weighing up a bunch of beautiful fresh vegetables

Having a "colonial princess" moment in Kerala

An Ayurvedic kitchen is full of beautiful vessels and essential utensils!

cooking, and find inspiration through my latest food safari. One of the most important things to remember when eating right for your shape is that Ayurvedic cooking and nutrition are more about guiding principles than strict rules. This isn't a restrictive fad diet like so many others endorsed in the Western world as a result of our reliance on processed foods and changing food systems. It's a balanced and considered approach to lifelong health, one that will give you complete control over the interplay of your bodily systems to keep your true self feeling balanced, healthy and calm.

HOW TO GET STARTED

In this book, I'll show you how to apply Ayurvedic principles to your life. Ayurveda is an ancient healing system, originating in India, that takes a holistic approach to feeling well and living in harmony with yourself and your surroundings.

It incorporates eating habits, digestion, daily routines, yoga and meditation. The emphasis is on balance, and one of the starting points is establishing your own particular dosha (or constitution: more on this on page 14), to enable you to tailor the principles to suit you.

Ayurveda is very simple to incorporate into your life without too much disruption. New things can seem hard, but sometimes all it takes is a little leap of faith. Don't worry about what other people might say; don't let labels and stereotypes stop you from walking to the beat of your own drum.

Starting a new way of eating and living that will benefit you internally and externally needn't be restrictive, complicated or difficult; it just needs to work for you. Your weight may be an unconquered facet of your life that you want to change. You may start to enjoy cooking and the healing benefits that food brings to your body. I hope you'll jump on board and experience this adventure with me to help find balance and happiness in your life.

Finding peace among the chaos of my Indian adventure

Meeting a yoga guru and experiencing a blissful yoga class in a beautiful hand-built studio

Erica and I wait on the platform to head to Thiruvananthapuram, as I build up the courage to board my first Indian train

To get started, it's a good idea to implement all diet and lifestyle changes gradually and not in a forceful way. Do little things as you start to understand the Ayurvedic approach and how to apply it to your life. Don't throw out all the food in your kitchen and try to cook new meals all in week one. You might just want to start with a yoga pose each day, then gradually work on other aspects of your life once you understand the best way for you and your lifestyle. Listening to your body and its needs is the key to integrating changes progressively, so that you can apply them and then subtly observe transformations and their effects. Remember, you are your own best teacher, guide and practitioner, and every small step you make will catapult you to the next level of wellness.

Becoming aware of how you feel and following your own path will serve you greatly when adopting Ayurvedic principles, so let go of comparing yourself to others, embrace your uniqueness, and follow your own path to healing and weight loss.

If you feel uncomfortable adopting a new food or lifestyle approach, just try something else instead – maybe down the track you'll take it up, so leave yourself open to new possibilities.

USING THIS BOOK

The first part of this book describes the Ayurvedic approach to life and has lots of practical advice on applying these principles so you can eat right for your own dosha and shape. Following that is a section on yoga poses and breathing exercises, and the last section has a mountain of delicious recipes for you to try. In the recipe section, you'll find symbols that remind you at a glance which dosha each recipe suits, and which of the six tastes each recipe incorporates (see page 35 for more on tastes). There's also a symbol telling you which recipes are useful during intermittent fasting (see page 56). These symbols are all explained on page 80.

PART 1

The Ayurvedic lifestyle

About Ayurveda

Ayurveda is a union of the mind, body, senses and soul. Through nutrition, yoga and meditation, it focuses on treating the individual as a whole rather than a specific issue or disease, so that you can achieve balance and good health, not only in your physical self, but also in your mind and spirit.

The practice of Ayurveda has three main objectives: to prevent disease, to encourage wellbeing and to promote longevity. These objectives are reached by applying four healing modalities to your life: eating nourishing food, engaging in cleansing and detoxification processes to purify the body while promoting weight loss, administering warm oil massages to eliminate energetic blockages in the body, and practicing yoga poses and meditation to create physical and emotional transformations.

By considering all the elements that make up your life, Ayurveda uncovers the root cause of illness to bring your body back into balance, and helps you understand yourself more fully. Through listening to your body and becoming aware of how to repair it and prevent disease, you can become your own best teacher and the architect of your future wellness.

One of the major differences between Ayurveda and modern medicine is somewhat philosophical, because in Ayurveda each individual is unique and no single approach or lifestyle routine will work for everyone. This comprehensive system enables you to treat yourself both as an individual and as a whole, so you can find the specific foods and daily routines that are balancing and healing for you.

Prevention is a key part of Ayurvedic practice, as it focuses on providing specific advice and guidance on how to maintain physical and emotional health. Instead of treatment with pharmaceutical drugs, this

Imagine walking into an Ayurvedic doctor's office with a complaint and coming out with a recipe rather than a prescription for medication. Food as preventative medicine is the future in our ailing healthcare system.

approach considers the food we eat and our lifestyle choices and routines to be the most important medicine we can feed our body.

A FLEXIBLE APPROACH

Ayurveda is a system that should enrich your life and not restrict it; that's why it's really important to take it slowly, enjoy the process and feel good about your food choices. It's not about rapid physical change or sudden extreme weight loss. There's no reason to put yourself on a strict regime and then fall off the wagon because it's too difficult to maintain. It's essential to not have an "I'm on a diet" mindset when making changes to your life. Being on a strict diet will only make you feel hungry and create powerful cravings for the very foods you're trying to avoid – generally foods like sugar, bad fats and processed foods. A sense of deprivation will only lead you to go off the rails and partake in rebellious overeating. Rigid plans can't sustain the ebb and flow of your state of health or withstand the pressures and triggers of everyday life. That's why it's good to make changes slowly, when you're ready, and not put too much pressure on yourself even if you do slip up. Think of additions rather than restrictions, and change the way you think about food. Even if you only follow Ayurvedic recipes one day a week, see this as a positive change.

THE IMPORTANCE OF MINDFULNESS

Create an internal environment where you can observe and understand yourself as much as possible. Learning how to listen to your body is paramount to being in harmony and balance. The mind and the body are connected in Ayurvedic philosophy, so the cultivation of self-reflection enables us to make decisions based upon comprehension and insight. When we're mindful, we observe our thoughts, emotions and sensations without judging them as good or bad, and this is an excellent tool you can apply to eating right for your shape. By cultivating mindfulness (see page 53), you'll begin to experience a state of awareness from which a sense of wellbeing and satiation blossoms. The emotional cravings will disappear and you'll be immersed in feelings of fullness.

DOSHAS

Doshas are energies that circulate around your body and govern physiological activity; they also determine your individual temperament and specific physical characteristics. There are three doshas – vata, pitta and kapha – and they're made up of the five elements – air, water, fire, earth and ether – that constitute our nature. When doshas are out of whack, they can cause physical and mental disorders. Finding your dominant dosha and keeping it in balance is the key to maintaining your weight and your overall health.

Establishing your principal dosha is the first step toward improving your health and reaching your wellness goals, whether these are simply to increase energy, improve a specific condition, lose weight or overcome particular health anxieties.

>>> — *Supercharged tip* — <<<

If you'd like to read more about the ancient practice of Ayurveda, there are plenty of great resources on the web.

Taking an Ayurvedic path in life will mean slowly implementing routines and dietary guidelines that cater specifically for your constitution and help you maintain the shape you should be. This is done by finding out your principal dosha (see page 14) and working on your doshic imbalances through the particular diet and lifestyle changes covered in this book. When your doshas are balanced, you will enjoy optimum health, stabilize your weight and radiate natural energy.

Finding your dosha

Take the dosha quiz to find out your dominant type. Once you've established your own dosha, you can start fine-tuning your diet to balance that dosha. Look through the list of foods and lifestyle suggestions on the following pages, and start incorporating them into your life. If you're kapha-dominant, the Ayurvedic diet will introduce more warmed foods and fewer cold foods; if you're mainly pitta, then cooling, raw foods will work best for you; and if your overriding dosha is vata, then warming foods are optimal.

THE DOSHA QUIZ

By taking into account your physical characteristics and your nature, this quiz will help you determine your dominant dosha: vata, pitta, kapha, or perhaps a combination of two, or even an equal combination of all three. Taking the quiz can help you identify and fine-tune your Ayurvedic constitution, and you can use this information to make diet and lifestyle choices that will help you reach your goals and intentions.

For each characteristic in the table opposite, choose which of the three options best describes you. Just try to be as honest as you can when choosing an alternative, and focus on your overall natural tendencies rather than how you might be feeling right now. Make a note at the bottom of each column of how many answers you have chosen in that column.

VATA   PITTA   KAPHA

Which dosha are you?
If most of your answers are in one column, that indicates your dominant dosha. If you have none or a few in one column but a more or less equal number in the other two, then you're vata–pitta, pitta–kapha or vata–kapha. If you have roughly equal numbers of all three, you're one of the rare vata–pitta–kaphas.

OBSERVATIONS	VATA	PITTA	KAPHA
Body size	Thin build	Medium build	Large build
Body weight	Low	Medium	Heavy
Weight change	Have trouble gaining weight	Gain weight but can lose it quickly	Easily gain weight and find it difficult to lose
Skin	Dry, thin and often itchy	Combination skin that appears flushed	Thick or oily
Skin texture and color	Cold, rough, light	Warm, reddish, freckles or moles	Cool, pale
Hair	Dry, thin, brittle and knots easily	Straight, prone to hair loss	Thick, full, lustrous, wavy and slightly oily
Hair color	Brown or black	Blond, grey or red	Dark brown or black
Face shape	Oval	Triangular (pointed chin and prominent jawline)	Round
Teeth and gums	Big, roomy, sticking out, with thin gums	Medium-sized, soft, with tender gums	Healthy, white, with strong gums
Eyes	Small, often dry, slightly dull, sunken, active, frequently blinking	Medium-sized, sharp, penetrating, sensitive to light	Big, round, with full eyelashes, calm
Eye color	Black or brown	Bright grey, green or yellow/red	Blue
Hands	Generally dry, rough, with slender fingers and dry nails	Generally moist, pink, with medium fingers and soft nails	Generally firm, thick, with thick fingers and strong, smooth nails
Lips	Dry, cracked, with a black or brown tint	Often inflamed, red or yellowish	Smooth, large, pale
Belly button	Small, irregular	Oval, superficial	Big, deep, round
Chest	Small, flat	Moderate	Broad
Joints	Small, with prominent bones, often crack	Medium and loose	Large, sturdy, with lots of surrounding muscle
Appetite	Irregular in frequency and size	Strong – cannot skip meals	Steady, regular, can skip meals
Taste	Sweet, sour, salty	Sweet, bitter, astringent	Bitter, pungent, astringent
Thirst	Variable	Sweet, bitter, astringent	Bitter, pungent, astringent
Digestion	Irregular	Quick	Slow
Physical activity	Very active (always on the go, mind constantly thinking)	Likes to think before doing anything	Steady and graceful (doesn't like to rush)
Personality	Vivacious, talkative, social, outgoing	Likes to be in control, intense, ambitious	Reserved, laid-back, concerned
Environment	Easily feels cold	Intolerant of heat	Uncomfortable in humidity
Sleep	Short, broken	Moderate and sound	Deep and long
Memory	Good in the short term, quick to forget	Medium but accurate	Slow to remember but then sustained
Financial	Buys on impulse	Spends money on luxuries	Good at saving money
Career preference	Creative arts, designing	Science or engineering	Management, human relations, care-giving

Score out of 27

UNDERSTANDING THE DOSHAS

Ayurveda classifies people into three main categories according to their constitution or *prakruti*, which relates to their genetically inherited physical, mental and emotional qualities, laid down at the moment of conception. *Prakruti* is made up of a combination of the three doshas – vata, pitta and kapha – and these can be roughly interpreted as representing the qualities of air, fire and earth respectively.

VATA air – cold, dry, light and mobile

PITTA fire – warm, oily and intense

KAPHA earth – damp and slow

We all have each one of the three doshas as part of our constitution and usually one or two dominate, but the proportions are unique in each of us.

Dosha proportions determine your physiological and personality traits, characteristics and preferences. If you're a vata (i.e. vata-dominant) like me, for example, you'd prefer a hot climate to a cold one, because vata characteristics are cold and a vacation in a warm place would bring this into balance. If you're a pitta, then cooling foods and juices would work for you. If you're a kapha, you'll be slow by nature and might therefore crave spicy foods to bring yourself into balance.

In Ayurveda, there are seven types of *prakruti*, depending on which dosha (or doshas) is dominant: **vata**, **pitta**, **kapha**, **vata–pitta**, **pitta–kapha**, **vata–kapha** and **vata–pitta–kapha**. Many of us have a dominant dosha. As I said, I'm vata-dominant, but some people have two equally dominant doshas (bi-doshic) and, in rare cases, some have all three doshas in equal proportions (tri-doshic).

The condition of our *prakruti* changes throughout our life for various reasons: an unhealthy diet and poor nutrition, emotional upsets and imbalances, an overload of stress or anxiety and/or a lack of physical activity. While each dosha plays an individual role in our body, complete wellness is only achieved when all three are in balance. Once you have an understanding of your dominant dosha and your unique proportions of vata, pitta and kapha, you'll be able to correct these imbalances and enable your body to feel calm, relaxed and in shape, but best of all in harmony.

WHAT IF ONE DOSHA IS NOT DOMINANT FOR YOU?

We're all mixtures of doshas, but for most of us one dosha will usually dominate, which means we can follow the advice for that dominant dosha most of the time. Occasionally, though, we may find that our secondary dosha is high. A vata-dominant, for example, might come home from work one day and realize that their pitta is high – they're feeling stressed or overheated. In this case they should choose foods that will bring their pitta into balance.

If you have an equal quantity of two doshas – you're bi-doshic – or a balanced blend of all three doshas – you're tri-doshic – then eat according to the daily lifestyle factors you're experiencing and in line with the seasons.

If you're bi-doshic, you may be feeling split. In times of stress or change, one dosha may dominate. If you're a vata–pitta or vata–kapha dosha, during autumn (which is a vata season) you should try to decrease the amount of vata. In effect, this means you'd be following a higher pitta or kapha diet during that season. This is how to manage a bi-doshic *prakruti* through the seasons.

A tri-doshic person can be very stable, robust and sturdy when in balance, but when out of balance their characteristics can become unstable and rigid. If you're tri-doshic, it's important to listen intently to your body and home in on its signals arising from emotional, environmental or dietary imbalances, and then use counterbalancing strategies to bring your body back on an even keel. For example, following a pitta-balancing regimen in summer (a pitta season) and a vata-based approach in autumn will help balance the three doshas.

Dosha characteristics

Here you'll find the characteristics and qualities of each dosha so that you can tailor your diet and lifestyle to suit. Each description covers personality, physical characteristics, diet and nutrition, how to balance your dosha, and dietary and lifestyle recommendations.

VATA

Vata types are creative and contagiously energetic. They make good teachers, artists, actors and professional speakers. The elements that govern vata are air and ether and, just like the wind, they can quickly get out of and back into balance. Vata is referred to as the 'king of the doshas' because it's responsible for every movement in the body. Its qualities are dry, light, cold, mobile and rough.

Personality

Vatas tend to talk a lot and worry a lot, too. They're usually on the move and find it hard to sit still. This is because of their elements of air and wind, so it's important for vatas to ground themselves and come back down to earth. They have a tendency to change their minds often and to run late, so a sense of calmness and keeping a regular routine are important. Some of the best balancing and nourishing activities for a vata constitution are meditation, gentle yoga practice and breathing.

Physical characteristics

Vatas tend to feel the cold, are prone to dry skin and can brown in the sun easily. They are slender in build and their hair is usually dry and curly.

Their face shape is generally oval and their eyes are small. They have long fingers and their nails can be brittle and easily broken. They can suffer from poor circulation and muscular aches and pains. Vatas benefit from steam rooms and daily naps between 2 pm and 4 pm. Physical ailments can be connected to the air element: vatas often suffer from such conditions as emphysema, pneumonia and arthritis.

Diet and nutrition

Nutritionally, vatas benefit from a diet high in good fats and oils, such as coconut oil and ghee. They prefer cooked vegetables and warming foods so they can stay oiled and content. Their digestion can be sluggish, and they can suffer from constipation, so a well-oiled diet helps lubricate their body and counterbalance their rough and dry qualities. Avoiding raw and cold foods helps balance them. Given vatas' irregular appetite and thirst, they often experience digestive problems and malabsorption.

Mindful eating

To achieve balance in their body weight, vatas should try to eat and sleep at the same time every night, and choose foods that are warm, cooked and easy to digest. Foods that balance vata include sweet berries and fruits; beans and brown rice; soaked or activated nuts (a small handful twice a week) and seeds; and oils (especially ghee). Avoid an overabundance of raw, cold, light and crunchy foods, which are too hard on the digestion.

How to balance vata

In balance, vata promotes creativity and flexibility. If vata is out of balance, fear and anxiety can result.

General guidelines for balancing vata

- Keep warm and avoid extreme cold.
- Eat a diet high in good fats.
- Consume warming foods and spices.
- Avoid cold, frozen or raw foods.
- Stay calm and grounded and get plenty of rest.
- Implement a regular routine.

Dietary recommendations for balancing vata

Vatas have a variable appetite and love to pick and graze throughout the day. To balance vata:

- Eat good quantities of grounding foods, such as quinoa and all types of nuts.
- Choose in-season, warming, grounding, mainly cooked foods that are sweet, salty and sour.
- Enjoy in moderation fruits that pacify vata, such as bananas, avocados, peaches, lemons, berries, coconut, rhubarb, nectarines, mangoes and plums. Avoid dried fruits, which are high in sugars and sulfites. To ease digestion, eat stewed fruits (like the Stewed Apple with Cloves recipe on page 196) on their own half an hour before other foods or two hours after other foods.
- Use good fats and oils, such as coconut oil, ghee and extra virgin olive oil to aid digestion.
- Minimize raw foods and eat cooked vegetables such as peas, winter squash, green beans, zucchini and sweet potatoes; and meats such as grass-fed lamb, organic chicken and seafood. Include eggs in your diet.
- Eat dairy foods; they pacify vata. Warming them up before eating them is better for your digestion.
- Use calming herbs and spices, such as cardamom, ginger, cumin, cinnamon, salt, cloves, asafoetida, basil, mustard seeds, cilantro, fennel, oregano, tarragon, thyme and black pepper.
- Sip warm water and drink warm herbal teas throughout the day to aid hydration. Try a tea of fresh ginger, cardamom and cinnamon to warm the body and enhance circulation and digestion.

Lifestyle recommendations for balancing vata

Prana, the vital life force, is the pure essence of vata.

- When you wake up each morning, do a few gentle yoga poses and a breathing exercise to bring awareness to your body. The cat–cow pose (see page 63) is a good one to start with, as it's a great grounding pose to prepare for the day ahead, while building strength and stability. Remember to focus on your breath. If you have time, include a breathing exercise after your routine such as alternate nostril breathing (see page 75) or a gentle meditation, then take a rest.
- After your morning shower or bath, massage your skin with a mixture of sesame oil and a healing essential oil such as ginger, lavender or rosewood.
- Try to find clothing that keeps you warm: layered garments made from soft natural fabrics such as cotton, linen and cashmere are perfect.
- Enjoy peaceful walks and gentle outdoor activity – being in nature helps calm and ground vata's mobility. Other suitable activities include gardening, art, music, writing and other creative pursuits. It's important to rest between activities, however.

Signs of balance in vata

Greater groundedness, clarity, calm and open-heartedness.

PITTA

Pittas are fiery people with leadership skills and intellect – they love a good debate! The elements that reign in pitta are fire and water. Pitta's qualities are sharp, hot, oily, smooth and mobile. Pitta heat is responsible for digestion and transformation of food, thoughts and physical exertion into energy. The state of your pitta digestive fire (*agni*) determines whether you are healthy and digesting your food properly. As pitta people are created from fire and water, they are sturdier than vata types. Pittas can get into and out of balance in a moderate amount of time.

Personality

Pittas have a competitive personality and do well in sport or a competitive environment. They have a sharp mind and are very good problem-solvers, but on the flip side can have a tendency to become overbearing, opinionated and controlling. They like to have things done a certain way, most often theirs, and like to have facts explained to them so that they can argue and cross-examine. Pittas make excellent lawyers and negotiators. They're extremely punctual and highly organized, and they adore making lists. When pittas are in balance, they are sharp and quick-witted, gregarious and humorous.

Physical characteristics

Pittas have an athletic build and their frame is medium-sized, well built and sturdy. Their skin is clear and toned, and can be reddish. Pittas are sensitive to the sun and can easily get sunburnt if not careful. They have sharp features and light-colored eyes. Their hair is fine, straight and thinning, and their fingernails are pink and strong. They sleep soundly for short periods and have a strong sex drive. As pittas are warm, they can display heat imbalances, such as fevers, inflammatory diseases, peptic ulcers and hypertension; and skin problems such as rashes and eczema.

Diet and nutrition

Pittas run hot, so it's important, both mentally and physically, for them to keep their diet as cool as possible. Breathing exercises help to cool pittas' fire. They respond well to sweet fruits and vegetables, salads, legumes, cucumber and cooling sweet treats such as coconut milk ice cream. Pittas should steer clear of excess salt, cheese, hot spices, sour fruits, yogurt and alcohol. Fortunately, pittas have a strong digestion and can eat a very varied diet. They tend to be hungry often and need to eat regularly or they become irritable and angry. No one likes an angry pitta! If pitta digestion is too sharp, it can result in diarrhea and increased acidity in the stomach, causing heartburn.

Mindful eating

To achieve stability, pittas require cooler foods, such as fresh vegetables and sweet watery fruits, especially cucumbers, celery and watermelon. They will also benefit from salads with dark leafy greens, such as kale, dandelion and arugula, and should avoid hot and spicy foods.

How to balance pitta

In balance, pitta aids intelligence and understanding. Out of balance, pitta produces anger and jealousy.

General guidelines for balancing pitta

- Stay away from excessive heat.
- Eat cooling, low-spice foods.
- Avoid excessive oil and limit salt intake.
- Exercise during the coolest part of the day.
- Steer clear of excessive steam.
- Meditate after 6 pm.

Dietary recommendations for balancing pitta

- Consume foods such as coconut, cucumber, watermelon and steamed greens. Eat fewer fermented products, as they aggravate pitta.
- Favor extra virgin coconut oil, the best oil for pacifying pitta. Avoid sesame, almond and corn oils, which are all warming.

- Eat foods that are cooling and calming; and sweet, bitter and astringent.
- Use soothing and cooling spices such as cilantro, cardamom, saffron and fennel.
- Include dairy in the form of butter and ghee.
- Eat barley and oats, the best grains to reduce pitta.
- Avoid corn, rye and millet.
- Consume sweet fruits such as grapes, melons, coconuts, avocados, mangoes, pomegranates, ripe pineapple and plums.
- Include more cooling vegetables, such as green leafy vegetables, asparagus, cucumbers, sweet potatoes, winter squash, broccoli, cauliflower, okra, lettuce, green beans and zucchini. Reduce your intake of tomatoes, chilies, eggplants, onions, garlic, radishes and spinach.
- For meat, eat mostly organic chicken and turkey, but you can also include grass-fed lamb and beef.
- Drink cool water and calming herbal teas, such as cilantro, fennel and rose, which will pacify heat and improve digestion.
- Never miss a meal, to avoid aggravating your system and mind.

Lifestyle recommendations for balancing pitta

- Many yoga poses (*asanas*) are beneficial, but the greatest balance comes from practicing in a relaxed way, focusing on your body rather than what's going on in your mind.
- When you're going through your morning routine, do so mindfully and with acceptance. It's a good idea to practice in a moderately cool space, and to avoid poses that create too much heat, as you don't want to get overheated. Incorporate poses that promote coolness, ease and lightness of being while releasing heat and stress in your small intestine, central abdomen, blood and liver.
- All forms of standing forward bends and inversions reduce pitta, so if you only do one yoga pose after waking up, make it a standing forward bend (see page 64). Working the abdominal area with twists can also be beneficial for pitta types.

- Emphasize a cooling breathing pattern during *asana* practice, where your exhale is longer than your inhale, and make a conscious effort to relax during the exhale. Most styles of meditation have a cooling quality, but these can be enhanced by incorporating cooling *mudras* (meditation positions), water imagery, or compassion or kindness meditation for overheated emotions such as deeply held anger, resentment or hatred. Throughout your practice, emphasize surrendering, forgiveness, softening and being gentle with yourself. Left-nostril breathing (see page 76) is a cooling exercise to try.
- Once you've had your morning shower or bath, massage your skin with extra virgin coconut oil.
- Try to opt for pale-colored, comfortable, cooling clothes in natural fabrics – cotton, linen and silk.
- Engage in water activities (such as swimming) and nature walks, which are extremely balancing.

Signs of balance in pitta

Reduced inflammation, acidity and irritation; greater coolness, calmness, openness, patience and tolerance.

KAPHA

Kapha people are steady, grounded and nurturing. They tend to be the healthiest of the three doshas, particularly when it comes to mental health. Kapha is the dosha responsible for the lubrication and structure of the body. Its elements are water and earth, and its governing qualities are wet, cold, heavy, oily and static. Kapha is our lubrication in the brain, joints and reproductive fluids, and is responsible for building tissue. Kaphas like to be in their comfort zone, and once they find a place where they're content, they find it hard to move. They don't like change or disruption, and like to stay where they are.

Personality
Kaphas are peacemakers and extremely popular. They listen and nurture, and like to help others. They're extremely tolerant and patient, and can form strong attachments. They're not easily upset, but if you do tip them over the edge, expect them to hold a grudge. They're sturdy, steady and reliable people who are genuinely happy.

Physical characteristics
Kaphas have a larger, well-built frame in even proportions, as well as strong joints, thick skin and strong bones. Their skin is clear, with large pores; and their eyes are moist and prominent, with long, full and curly eyelashes. Their lips are full and they have large strong teeth. Their hair is thick, lustrous and usually wavy, and they feel cool and moist to the touch. They have a strong immune system and great endurance. They sleep well and deeply for long periods and tend to gain weight easily. Kaphas are prone to static and heavy conditions such as obesity, lethargy, diabetes and dullness of mind. They also suffer from physical ailments connected to the water element, such as colds and flu, sinus congestion and excess mucus. Regular saunas are very beneficial for kaphas.

Diet and nutrition
Kaphas are cold, heavy and static, so they find keeping dry and light and getting moving beneficial. Because their appetite and metabolism are slow, a light diet is best, and fasting benefits them and increases their digestive fire (*agni*). As kapha is made up of water and earth, they should eat airy and dry foods, such as vegetables, fruits, salads and legumes, as well as warm and spicy foods.

Mindful eating
Kaphas need light, warm, spicy foods that reduce sluggishness, depression and weight gain, such as fresh ginger and lemon tea. They should avoid oily foods and processed sugars, favoring spices such as ginger, black pepper, cumin and chili. For weight loss they should eat dark bitter greens.

How to balance kapha
Kapha in balance creates calmness and forgiveness. Out of balance, kapha produces greed and envy.

General guidelines for balancing kapha
- Stay active and get plenty of exercise.
- Vary your routine.
- Eat light meals.
- Avoid heavy foods, dairy and fatty, oily foods.
- Don't consume iced foods and drinks.
- Steer clear of daytime naps.

Dietary recommendations for balancing kapha
- Fast on two separate days each week (see page 56), eating no more than 500 calories. Eat Kitchari (see page 261), soups, vegetable juices and smoothies, try the fasting recipes on pages 256–7 and check for the fasting symbol on other recipes.
- Reduce your intake of dairy, which tends to aggravate kapha. Sheep's or goat's milk products are better options.
- For sweeteners, use rice malt syrup, stevia and pure raw honey, all of which pacify kapha.

- Avoid foods that cause mucus accumulation, such as cheese and ice cream, and gravitate toward foods that are warming and stimulating.
- Use only small amounts of extra virgin olive oil, ghee, almond oil and coconut oil.
- Drink two to three cups of hot ginger tea daily, with meals, to help stimulate digestion and sharpen dull tastebuds.
- Indulge in lighter fruits such as apples, pears, pomegranates, cranberries and apricots, and reduce your intake of heavier fruits such as bananas, avocados, pineapples, oranges, peaches, coconuts, melons, dates and figs.
- Use pungent spices such as black pepper, cayenne pepper, mustard seeds and ginger freely in your diet. All spices except salt will pacify kapha.
- Reduce your intake of nuts and seeds, though you can eat pecans, walnuts, pumpkin seeds and sunflower seeds in moderation.
- Eat moderate amounts of organic white meat, such as chicken, turkey and seafood, and grass-fed red meats. Eggs are also acceptable.
- Eat your largest meal at lunchtime and a smaller meal at dinnertime. Allow your dinner at least three hours to digest before going to bed.
- Eat barley, millet, buckwheat and rye, but reduce your intake of rice and wheat.
- To increase your circulation and eliminate mucus, drink warm herbal teas such as one with ginger, cinnamon and a pinch of ground cloves.

Lifestyle recommendations for balancing kapha
Kaphas need attachment, so they should practice detachment from people, emotional upsets, home comforts and material possessions.
- Move energetically and create flow around your body. Make a firm commitment to maintaining a non-sedentary life and staying motivated. The areas of the body related to kapha are the lungs and stomach/diaphragm area. To balance kapha, do heart-opening poses that concentrate on opening the chest. These will help stretch the throat, relieve congestion and drain the sinuses.
- Choose kapha-reducing standing yoga poses such as standing forward bend (see page 64), triangle (see page 66) and warrior II (see page 65), which all promote endurance. It's good to have a varied routine, so try at least three different poses each morning and rotate them. Do a rigorous practice, to work up a good sweat.
- Work the lungs with heating *ujjayi* breathing (deep breathing; see page 76). This is extremely beneficial, as is right-nostril breathing (see page 76), which is cleansing, energizing, warming and also promotes good circulation. Follow the breathing exercise with quiet meditation.
- Before your morning shower or bath, do whole-body dry skin brushing to promote circulation. Try sea salt scrubs or essential oils (such as grapefruit and cypress) that are uplifting, decrease edema and increase lymph circulation.
- Wear warm clothes in fabrics such as denim, wool and cashmere. Keep your head and neck warm during winter with a knit cap and scarf.
- Try not to take naps, especially during winter, as this slows down the metabolism and reduces the fire necessary for digestion and weight loss.

Signs of balance in kapha
Weight normalisation; elimination of excess congestion, mucus and water; a greater sense of detachment.

Making it work for your family

Say you're a kapha but your partner is a vata and your daughter is a pitta. How on earth do you cook an evening meal while keeping everyone in balance and not feeling like a short-order cook? There's no point bringing yourself into balance if it will send everyone else out of whack. Then everyone will be stressed and confused!

You might start to feel like a juggler with a flaming torch in one hand and a chainsaw in the other, but it doesn't have to be that way and you don't need to join the circus just yet!

If this is your situation, take into account the alternatives I've provided for each dosha as you plan your meals, and use herbs to alter the recipes slightly. You might want to cook a curry, for example. While a nice hot curry will be perfect for your partner and you, you'll need to make it mild for your daughter and then later add more spices for you and your partner. Serve your daughter's with a salad and, if necessary for balance, serve yours and your partner's with the churna masala (spice mix; see page 238) for your particular doshas. When in doubt, cook for the person who is the most out of balance.

Ease into it slowly: start by preparing one Ayurvedic meal per week. Once you and your family realize the food tastes fantastic, add a couple more dishes to your weekly meal planning. If your family is used to processed foods, the benefits of an Ayurvedic lifestyle will quickly show in everyone's health and energy levels. At the very least, try to eat seasonally and locally, include wholefoods in your diet and keep it simple.

Get your family involved in choosing, preparing and cooking the meals together, with one of the highest Ayurvedic philosophies – love!

What shape are you?

In our modern world, weight problems and associated lifestyle diseases are skyrocketing. The big problem is that quick-fix, one-size-fits-all weight-loss solutions will constantly let people down, as they fail to acknowledge that we each have individual and unique needs. The Ayurvedic approach to health offers a more holistic, uniquely tailored way of achieving your ideal weight by eating right for your shape or dosha.

There are four common body types, one of which will characterize your shape: banana, pear, apple and hourglass. This is the natural body shape you're born with, but it can change according to your lifestyle. You may be a vata but have increased weight and so may look like a kapha. Eat according to the body shape you were born with.

By choosing a lifestyle that balances your unique type, you'll find you can achieve great success in rectifying the common weight issues associated with your body shape.

In the next section, you'll find an abundance of scrumptious recipes, each one classified according to which dosha (and therefore which body shape) it is suitable for.

Banana – vata

Bananas naturally maintain a long, thin, linear shape with a narrow waist, hips and shoulders, and longer limbs. They're lucky enough to find it difficult to gain weight, but when their dosha is out of balance, they can put on weight around their stomach and lower half of their body, leading to heart problems and slowed organ function, both of which can result in the accumulation of toxins.

In Ayurvedic medicine, the banana shape falls into the vata dosha. The vata's constitution is predominantly "air", requiring a balance of fiery, warming, heavier lifestyle choices to maintain balanced weight. If you're a banana, your diet should include warming spices such as cayenne pepper, ginger and black pepper; heavier fruits such as avocados, papayas and mangoes; and root vegetables. These foods will add more fire to your digestion, helping to remove toxins. One perfect recipe for a banana would be the Stewed Fruits with Cashew Cream (page 97).

For fitness, choose more heating activities, such as weight training, or yoga styles where the poses are held longer to build fire and strength.

Pear – pitta

Pear shapes have quite strong, athletic bodies, but will gain weight around the hips, buttocks and thighs, resulting in cellulite and varicose veins. Pears fall within the pitta dosha, representing fire and strength. Unfortunately, our society is very fiery by nature, regularly throwing pittas out of balance and leading them to gain weight from stress and overeating. If you're a pear, you therefore require a cooling diet with loads of fresh, raw vegetables, fruits and plenty of water. Green vegetable juices rich in chlorophyll will help oxygenate your blood and boost your circulation, clearing the build-up of toxins that leads to cellulite.

Long-distance exercises focusing on the lower half, such as gentle jogging, walking and swimming, are perfect for the pitta who wants to become leaner.

Apple – kapha

Apples tend to gain weight easily around the middle, which can suffocate their organs, stress their body and lead to high levels of cortisol (the stress hormone), diabetes and inflammation.

They fall into the kapha dosha, which represents water and heaviness. Apple shapes therefore require "fiery" lifestyle choices to pick up their metabolism, burn fat around their middle and improve their digestion. They should eat airy foods such as apples and broccoli, as well as grapefruits and lemons, which are highly detoxifying and help boost circulation.

Styles of yoga such as *vinyasa* (flow yoga), and high-intensity activities such as weight training and running, are perfect to combat the apple's heaviness around the middle.

Hourglass – pitta–kapha

The often-envied hourglass shape is not without its troubles. Although well proportioned on the top and bottom, with a small waist, they can gain excessive weight on their thighs, as well as their back and shoulders – a double whammy!

Hourglasses fall within both the pitta and kapha doshas, and so require a balance of the two Ayurvedic lifestyles described for pears and apples. Light and cooling foods such as raw veggies and fruits are great for pitta–kaphas.

A combination of strength training and grounding yoga will help target the pitta–kapha's whole body to avoid fat and toxic build-up in their upper and lower halves.

FOODS FOR VATAS TO EAT

Vata is cold, light, dry, dynamic and ever-changing. If you have a vata dosha, choose foods that are warming, oily, heavy, sweet, salty and sour to help ground you and bring you stability. Eat fruits liberally. You'll find vegetables especially nourishing when they're cooked in ghee or coconut oil with warming spices.

VEGETABLES

Beets	Sweet potato
Carrots	Turnips
Fennel	Watercress
French shallots	Zucchini
Garlic	
Green beans	
Green chilies	
Leeks	
Peas	
Rutabega	
Sea vegetables	
Snow peas	
Squash	

FRUITS

Apples (cooked)	Mangoes
Apricots	Melons
Avocados	Mulberries
Bananas	Nectarines
Blackberries	Olives
Blueberries	Oranges
Cherries	Papayas
Coconuts and coconut products	Peaches
Dates (soaked)	Persimmons
Figs	Pineapples
Goji berries	Plums
Grapefruit	Raisins
Grapes	Raspberries
Kiwifruit	Rhubarb
Lemons	Strawberries
Limes	Tamarind

GRAINS AND FLOURS

Basmati rice	Sorghum
Brown rice	Spelt
Oats, oat flour and oatmeal	Tapioca
Quinoa	Whole wheat
Rice flour	Wild rice

LEGUMES

Tempeh	Tofu

SEEDS, NUTS AND NUT BUTTERS

Almond butter	Pepitas (pumpkin seeds)
Almonds	Pine nuts
Chia seeds	Poppy seeds
Flaxseeds (linseed)	Sesame seeds
Hazelnuts	Sunflower seeds
Hemp seeds	

MEAT, FISH AND EGGS

Beef	Freshwater fish
Chicken	Lamb in moderation
Eggs	Turkey

DAIRY, DAIRY ALTERNATIVES AND DRINKS

Almond milk
Blue cheese
Cheddar cheese
Coconut cream
Coconut milk
Cottage cheese
Cow's milk
Cream
Goat's cheese
Goat's milk
Kefir
Kombucha
Mozzarella
Oat milk
Parmesan
Rice milk
Romano cheese
Sour cream
Yogurt

FATS, OILS AND CONDIMENTS

Animal fat (tallow, lard)
Apple cider vinegar
Butter
Cacao butter
Coconut butter
Coconut oil
Flaxseed oil
Ghee
Mayonnaise, homemade
Miso
Mustard
Olive oil
Pickles
Safflower oil
Sauerkraut
Sesame oil
Sunflower oil
Tahini
Tamari

SWEETENERS

Coconut sugar
Maple syrup
Molasses
Rapadura sugar (panela, jaggery)
Rice malt syrup (brown rice syrup)
Stevia
Vanilla beans

HERBS AND SPICES

Allspice
Asafoetida
Basil
Bay leaves
Black pepper
Caraway seeds
Cardamom
Cayenne pepper
Chili, fresh, dried and powdered
Chives
Cilantro
Cinnamon
Cloves
Cumin
Curry leaves
Curry powder
Dill
Dulse flakes
Fennel seeds
Fenugreek
Ginger
Marjoram
Mustard seeds and powder
Nigella seeds (charnushka)
Nutmeg
Oregano
Paprika
Parsley
Rosemary
Saffron
Sea salt
Star anise
Tarragon
Thyme
Turmeric

FOODS FOR PITTAS TO EAT

Pitta is sharp, fiery, light and intense. People with a pitta dosha will benefit greatly from an abundance of raw, cooling, sweet foods that will stabilize a fiery body and mind. An abundance of soothing and cooling vegetables and sweet juicy fruits are especially nourishing for pittas.

VEGETABLES

Alfalfa sprouts	Mushrooms
Arugula	Okra
Asparagus	Onions
Bean sprouts	Potatoes
Beets	Red-leaf lettuce
Broccoli	Romaine lettuce
Cabbage	Rutabega
Carrots	Snow peas
Cauliflower	Squash
Chicory lettuce	Sweet potato
Collard greens	Swiss chard
Cucumbers	Turnips
French shallots	Zucchini
Green beans	
Green onions	
Jerusalem artichokes	
Kale	
Kohlrabi	
Leeks	

FRUITS

Apples	Guavas
Avocados	Lemon zest
Bananas	Limes
Bitter melons	Melons
Blackberries	Mulberries
Blueberries	Peaches
Coconut products, not coconuts themselves	Persimmons
Cranberries	Pineapples
Currants	Pomegranates
Dates	Prunes
Figs	Raisins
Goji berries	Raspberries
Grapes	Rhubarb
Green mangoes	Strawberries
	Watermelons

GRAINS AND FLOURS

Amaranth	Sorghum
Barley	Spelt
Basmati rice	Tapioca
Oats, oat bran, oatmeal and oat flour	Wheat
Puffed rice	White rice flour
Quinoa	Wild rice

LEGUMES

Adzuki beans
Black beans
Black-eyed peas
Broad (fava) beans
Butter beans
Cannellini beans
Chickpeas
  (garbanzo beans)
Kidney beans
Lentils

Mung beans
Navy beans
Pinto beans
Soya beans
  and edamame
Split peas
Tempeh
Tofu
Urad dal

SEEDS, NUTS AND NUT BUTTERS

Almond butter
Almonds
Brazil nuts
Chia seeds
Flaxseeds (linseed)

Hemp seeds
Macadamias
Pepitas (pumpkin seeds)
Poppy seeds
Sunflower seeds

MEAT, FISH AND EGGS

Beef
Chicken
Egg whites
Freshwater fish

Lamb in moderation
Pheasant
Turkey

DAIRY, DAIRY ALTERNATIVES AND DRINKS

Almond milk
Butter, unsalted
Coconut cream

Cow's milk
Oat milk

FATS, OILS AND CONDIMENTS

Cacao butter
Coconut butter
Coconut oil

Flaxseed oil
Ghee
Mayonnaise, homemade

SWEETENERS

Coconut sugar
Maple syrup
Pomegranate
  molasses
Rapadura sugar
  (panela, jaggery)

Rice malt syrup
  (brown rice syrup)
Stevia
Vanilla beans

HERBS AND SPICES

Burdock
Cardamom
Chamomile
Cilantro,
  fresh, dried
  and seeds
Dandelion

Dulse flakes
Fennel seeds
Ginger, fresh only
Green tea
Lavender
Mint
Saffron

(Pittas can use turmeric, cumin, black pepper, Chinese cinnamon, dill and sweet orange zest in moderation)

FOODS FOR KAPHAS TO EAT

Kapha is naturally slow, heavy, wet, cool, soft and oily. To avoid imbalance, people with a kapha dosha need to stay away from foods with these characteristics, especially dairy. The best dietary options for kaphas include sharp, hot, dry, pungent, bitter and astringent foods, such as herbs, spices, legumes and bitter greens.

VEGETABLES

Alfalfa sprouts	Kale
Artichokes	Kohlrabi
Arugula	Leeks
Asparagus	Mushrooms
Bean sprouts	Okra
Beet greens	Parsnips
Beets	Peas
Broccoli	Potatoes
Brussels sprouts	Radishes
Cabbage	Red bell peppers
Cauliflower	Red-leaf lettuce
Celery	Red onion
Chicory	Romaine lettuce
Chilies	Spaghetti squash
Corn	Sweet potato
Eggplant	Swiss chard
Endive	Turnips
Fennel	Turnip greens
French shallots	Watercress
Garlic	
Green beans	
Green chilies	
Jalapeño chilies	
Jerusalem artichokes	

FRUITS

Apples	Limes
Apricots (fresh)	Oranges
Bitter melons	Pears
Cherries	Pomegranates
Cranberries	Prunes
Goji berries	Rhubarb
Grapefruit	Strawberries
Green mangoes	Tomatoes
Lemons	Watermelons

GRAINS AND FLOURS

Amaranth	Sorghum
Barley	Spelt
Basmati rice	Tapioca
Oats, oat bran,	Wheat
oatmeal and oat flour	White rice flour
Puffed rice	Wild rice
Quinoa	

LEGUMES

Adzuki beans	Lentils
Black beans	Mung beans
Black-eyed peas	Navy beans
Broad (fava) beans	Pinto beans
Butter beans	Soya beans and
Cannellini beans	edamame
Chickpeas	Split peas
Kidney beans	Urad dal

SEEDS, NUTS AND NUT BUTTERS

Pecans	Sesame seeds
Pepitas (pumpkin seeds)	Walnuts

(Kaphas can have chia seeds in moderation)

MEAT, FISH AND EGGS

Chicken	Lamb in moderation
Egg whites	Turkey
Freshwater fish	

DAIRY, DAIRY ALTERNATIVES AND DRINKS

Rice milk

FATS, OILS AND CONDIMENTS

Apple cider vinegar	Sesame oil
Mustard	Spirulina
Mustard oil	Tamari
Safflower oil	

(Kaphas can have small quantities of olive oil, ghee, almond oil and coconut oil)

SWEETENERS

Cacao	Stevia
Carob	Vanilla extract
Raw honey, unheated	

HERBS AND SPICES

Allspice	Fennel seeds
Basil	Fenugreek
Bay leaves	Ginger
Black pepper	Green tea
Black tea	Horseradish
Burdock	Lavender
Caraway seeds	Lemongrass
Cardamom	Marjoram
Cayenne pepper	Mint
Celery seeds	Mustard powder
Chamomile	and seeds
Chickweed	Nigella seeds
Chili powder	(charnushka)
and flakes	Oregano
Chives	Paprika
Cilantro	Parsley
Coriander	Rosemary
Cumin	Saffron
Curry leaves	Sage
Curry powder	Star anise
Dandelion	Tarragon
Dill	Thyme
Dulse flakes	Turmeric

The six tastes and your dosha

Food is vital and central to Ayurvedic medicine, and its nutritional wisdom quite literally rests upon the tip of your tongue. Our tastebuds not only identify and discriminate between the flavor hits we encounter when we eat, they also unlock the nutritive value of foods and kick-start the entire digestive process. Any substance with which your body comes into contact will either aggravate or pacify your dosha.

An Ayurvedic approach to eating includes all six tastes: sweet, sour, salty, bitter, pungent and astringent. Just as each dosha correlates with a combination of two of the five elements – earth, air, fire, water and ether – each taste is comprised of two elements.

BALANCING THE SIX TASTES

Operating on the theory that "like increases like", an Ayurvedic approach to the senses of taste (or *rasa*) includes choosing those with qualities that are the opposite of your doshic imbalance, in order to create harmony and health. The six tastes offer us a road map for complete nourishment and equilibrium within our body, so rather than studying food labels and the number of calories or carbohydrates in a particular food, following the six tastes will naturally guide you toward what your body needs. By understanding the way each taste affects your dosha, you can choose foods and herbs that will create balance and healing for your individual constitution and satisfy you at each meal.

Your brain sends signals to your body when it's hungry. Tuning in to the requirements of your unique constitution will allow you to make better choices about the proportion of tastes you combine in a meal. Having the correct proportion of all six tastes and satisfying your body's signals will help you avoid the cravings and overeating that lead to weight gain. If, for example, you are a kapha, you may need to add more greens to a recipe for the astringent qualities they bring, and reduce the sweetness or saltiness.

When we listen to our inner voice and tune in naturally to the tastes we desire, we tap into our body's innate wisdom for healing.

This guide will help you understand the effects certain tastes will have on your unique constitution, so you can begin to choose foods that will bring you into balance. For complete nourishment, Ayurveda states that all the important nutrients required for life, such as fats, proteins, carbohydrates, minerals and vitamins, are contained in a meal that consists of all six tastes combined. It's not hard to incorporate the six different tastes into your meals. It might just mean adding a squeeze of lime or lemon to add a sour element, or scattering cilantro over a meal to add sweet and astringent tastes.

Which tastes are best for you?

Dosha	Most balancing	Most aggravating
Vata	Sweet, sour, salty	Bitter, pungent, astringent
Pitta	Sweet, bitter, astringent	Sour, salty, pungent
Kapha	Pungent, bitter, astringent	Sweet, sour, salty

Sweet (madhura)

Earth and water: heavy, moist, oily and cooling

In the right balance, sweetness promotes energy, stability and vitality. Sweet is balancing for both vata and pitta, grounding airy vata's nervous energy and soothing pitta's aggravated digestive fire with its cool watery nature while promoting a healthy body mass.

Sweetness aggravates kapha, promoting mucus, congestion, coughs, heaviness and lethargy. Because sweet tastes naturally increase bulk, moisture and weight in the body, kaphas pursuing weight loss should decrease their intake of sweet foods.

Obvious sweet foods include dates, rice malt syrup, maple syrup and most fruits. More subtly, sweetness is a feature of butter, ghee, milk, macadamias, almonds, cashews, coconut products, carrots, sweet potatoes and fish.

Sour (amla)

Earth and fire: heavy and warming

Sour brings many benefits, including stimulation of salivary secretions, appetite, digestion and elimination. Psychologically, it enlivens the mind and sharpens the senses, enhancing both critical thinking and comprehension. Sour also helps us extract minerals such as iron from food.

Sour will pacify vata and can aggravate pitta and kapha. Vatas will notice that sour foods stimulate their delicate digestion, while pittas will find that these foods leave them inundated with too much heat, which fires up their digestion and causes reflux and gut inflammation. An excess of sour for kaphas will promote heaviness due to water retention.

Sour foods include lemons, limes, vinegars, yogurt, sauerkraut and fermented vegetables, pickles and berries.

Salty (lavana)

Water and fire: heavy, moist and heating

Salt is a vital substance that gives energy, promotes growth, balances electrolytes, enhances appetite and makes flavors more delicious. Emotionally, it enhances the flavor of life, sparks interest and enthusiasm, builds courage and raises confidence.

Salty tastes will balance vata and can aggravate kapha and pitta. For vatas, salt will stimulate digestion, bringing warmth to the body and hydration to the organs and tissues. For already watery kaphas, it can lead to excessive fluid retention, weight gain and swelling. The fire element in salty foods will add too much heat to pitta, leading to hyperactivity and hypertension.

Use Himalayan and Celtic sea salts, which include a variety of trace minerals. Traditionally, salt is added at the end of the cooking process. Intrinsically salty foods include tamari, soy sauce, miso, nutritional yeast, salted meats and seaweeds.

Bitter (tikta)

Air and ether: cool, light, dry, empty, subtle and spacious

Bitter tastes contribute to purification, dehydration, waste removal and detoxification. They boast antibacterial and antiviral properties and, on a mental level, can promote the expansion of creativity, introspection and metacognition – the ability to think about your own thinking.

kapha. Vatas are sensitive to emotional imbalances, so the empty, absent nature of ether and air within bitter tastes means they make vatas prone to feelings of isolation, grief, loneliness and emptiness, and the physical health consequences that accompany these states. On the other hand, pitta is soothed and cooled by bitter tastes, which tame a fiery digestion and cleanse a toxic liver. For heavy kaphas, bitter foods will provide detoxification and reduce fat and water retention, making them important for kaphas who want to lose weight and eat right for their shape.

Bitterness is in dandelion, coffee, green and black tea; dense greens such as spinach, chicory, mustard greens, kale and collards; and other vegetables such as green cabbage, zucchini and eggplant. It is also in turmeric, fenugreek, olives, grapefruit and bitter melon.

Pungent (*katu*)

Fire and air: heating, light and drying

Pungent flavors in the right balance will help digestion and circulation, dissolve excess fat and eliminate it from the body, and increase enthusiasm, perception and mental clarity.

The dryness and lightness of pungent tastes make them beautifully pacifying for the kapha dosha, increasing circulation and digestion, removing toxic build-up in the organs and sparking much-needed enthusiasm and creativity in the mind. Pungency also improves metabolism and relieves muscle pain. Too much pungency will increase mental and physical irritation in vata, and will create inflammation in pitta.

Pungent foods include black pepper, ginger, chilies, onions, garlic, cloves and mustard.

Astringent (*kashaya*)

Air and earth: cooling, drying, firming and heavy

Astringent, the least common of the six tastes, is responsible for mental purification, centring, decongestion, fighting inflammation, and physical and emotional strength.

Astringent flavors will increase vata and decrease kapha and pitta. Due to the airiness of astringent foods, in vatas they can aggravate gas, indigestion, malabsorption, fear and anxiety. Kaphas will experience relief from weakness and limpness in the body, and drying relief to water retention and oily skin. Astringency cools pitta, decreasing inflammation, and bringing a sense of grounding and organization.

You'll find astringent flavors in legumes, broccoli, cauliflower, pomegranates, underripe fruits, alfalfa sprouts, green beans and okra.

Understanding the three gunas

Our food has an energy source, and the qualities of the energy that exists both in the universe and in the food we eat are known in Ayurveda as the gunas. These are:

sattva: lucidity, purity, balance, lightness and consciousness
rajas: activity, air, force and passion
tamas: darkness, inertia, obscurity, negativity, lethargy, dullness and sleepiness.

Think about your last meal and how the food made you feel afterward. It may be related to one guna or a combination of two. It's similar to your activities throughout the day. While a yoga class might put you into a sattvic state, staying home and sitting around all day would leave your mind in a tamasic state. Knowing this makes you more aware of the food you eat and the effect it has on your body and state of mind, so that you can eat more consciously.

A more sattvic diet will help keep you in balance. My Ayurvedic teacher explained how vegetables and plants that grow fast are heavier for the digestion, while those that take longer to grow are easier to digest. For example, raw Asian greens, peas and leafy herbs can be hard on the digestive system, while slow growers such as carrots, parsnips and sweet potatoes are easier to digest. It's a simple concept of food using single ingredients – such as one type of cooking fat – and simple combinations of ingredients.

Through understanding which foods agree with you and support you, you can develop the inner wisdom to eat right for your shape.

Sattva
Sattvic foods are full of *prana* (life force). Easy to digest and light, they can be naturally sweet, juicy and tasty, and don't produce toxins. They include foods such as easily digestible fresh fruit and vegetables; grains, seeds and nuts; dairy foods; olive, coconut and sesame oils; herbs and spices such as ginger, cinnamon, cardamom, turmeric, fennel and cilantro; and herbal teas.

Rajas
Rajasic foods are generally salty, hot, dry, bitter and sour, and have an accompanying strong taste. They raise activity and excitement levels, but can also elevate anxiety and fears. These include foods that are heated and contain stimulants, such as fried food, coffee and tea, spices, meat, garlic, onion, fermented foods, chocolate and sweet foods. They also include overripe and stale food. Rajasic foods support physical endurance but can irritate the body's immunity. Limiting your exposure to rajasic foods, people and situations – and increasing your exposure to sattvic foods, people and situations – will help you achieve harmony.

Tamas
Tamasic foods are lacking in *prana* and can make you feel lethargic. They include stale, old and leftover food, deep-fried food, and too much grain-fed meat, chicken or hard cheese. Certain herbs and spices, such as nutmeg, have a tamasic effect upon the mind, which is why nutmeg is used as a traditional relaxation aid. Tamasic foods require a lot of energy to digest and can make the mind gloomy.

Practicalities
Think of the gunas as a food pyramid. At the bottom, representing the foods you should eat most, sit sattvic foods. In the middle are rajasic foods – eat these as needed. And at the tip are tamasic foods – eat these only in small amounts. Put together your own food pyramid by considering the gunas of the foods that are best for your dosha (see pages 28–33).

The Ayurvedic kitchen

Although it's an ancient practice, Ayurvedic principles are still very much alive and well in kitchens all over India, as I saw first hand when I visited the country with my beautiful Indian friend Erica (who has generously shared one of her own delicious recipes, the Crumbed Fish with Sautéed Beans, on page 156).

Ayurvedic cooking emphasises the use of equipment that is as natural as possible rather than working with synthetic materials, which can pose a health risk.

Did you know, for example, that using plastic kitchen equipment can transfer plasticisers such as phthalates and dioctyl adipate straight into food? The migration of these plasticisers into your food is significantly increased when you add heat to the mix, and the fattier the food, the higher the contamination. These ingredients belong in a chemical laboratory, not in your body. Phthalates have been shown to exhibit hormone-like behaviors and are a suspected endocrine (hormone system) disruptor. Indians believe that women have a higher absorption rate because of their metabolism, so it's important to invest in safe cookware.

When decking out your Ayurvedic kitchen, stay away from any material that is plastic, aluminium, "non-stick" (Teflon-coated) or anodized, as these can all leach toxins into food and release toxic fumes when heated. Instead, opt for stainless steel, wood, cast iron, ceramic or glass utensils. Microwave ovens are also not recommended, due to their unnatural transformative effect on food.

Although different vessels are used for different situations, my go-to non-toxic cooking material is cast iron. It's generally cheaper than stainless steel, super sturdy and can be transferred from stovetop to oven. It boosts iron levels in the body, distributes heat evenly, creates beautiful browning and, when properly seasoned and cared for, is easy to clean without dishwashing liquid. Because cast iron is considered bitter and cold, using it to prepare heat-predominant food and heat-producing food, such as chili and spices, can be good for reducing pitta.

In Indian Ayurvedic kitchens, bronze and brass are used for multiple taste combinations – sweet, sour and salty – or when more than five vegetables or all the food groups are used. Bronze and brass are traditionally used when cooking for big groups.

Earthenware or clay is another traditional and safe option. Clay is astringent, and using it to cook anything grown below the earth – such as yams, carrots or potatoes – protects the fiber value of the food and increases digestible fiber. Making a tandoori in a clay oven can help kapha by reducing water content while maintaining fiber value.

In India, they believe that gold is the highest nourishing metal and used for the gods. When food is cooked in gold, its nutrient value isn't lost. Eating from a gold vessel with a gold spoon is considered the equivalent of a monarch wearing a crown.

THE EQUIPMENT YOU NEED

Transform your kitchen into an Ayurvedic food haven with these utensils:

- a small saucepan with a lid, for melting ghee, cooking rice or grains and heating individual meals
- a large saucepan with a lid, for larger meals, soups and stews
- a frying pan/skillet, for frying and sautéing
- a blender, for liquefying soups and smoothies
- a food processor, for convenient chopping and crumbing, and making curry pastes
- a mortar and pestle, for grinding herbs and spices
- a steamer or saucepan steaming attachment, for steaming veggies and other ingredients
- mixing bowls, measuring cups and spoons, for preparing wholefood Ayurvedic recipes
- glass jars and bottles, for storing homemade nut milks, dips, spreads and pantry ingredients instead of using plastic containers. These can also be used for packed lunches and smoothies on the go.
- a large sharp chef's knife and small sharp paring knife
- a whisk, for making omelettes and emulsifying dressings and liquid ingredients
- a soup ladle, for serving broths, soups and stews
- a wooden spatula, for flipping, sautéing and stirring
- a box grater, for cheese and salad ingredients
- a water filter, to provide toxin-free drinking and cooking water.

THE KITCHEN PHARMACY

When it comes to achieving true health, there's no one-size-fits-all approach. Thankfully, the Ayurvedic method of eating for your individual dosha acknowledges these differences, and provides you with a framework for cooking meals that support your unique needs.

Medicinal recipes have been passed down, and the particular foods required to balance out a dominant dosha, whether vata, pitta or kapha, are still well known and cooked regularly today.

Unlike modern pharmaceuticals, you can find these common ingredients in your pantry or buy them at low cost, without worrying about the risk of adverse side effects. The Ayurvedic world of culinary medicine is not just about curing illness, but supporting and bringing vitality to the whole person. Enjoying and mindfully engaging with the right foods for your dosha will bring a new level of joy and freedom to your health journey, resolving illness and weight issues naturally along the way.

Three vata medicine-chest must-haves

If your dominant dosha is vata, an imbalance will manifest itself in such symptoms as weight loss, anxiety, viral illnesses, constipation and irregular bowel movements. This imbalance can be pacified through sweet, sour and salty tastes. Mild spices are wonderful for fuelling the digestive fire (*agni*) needed for a balanced metabolism. Using ginger in tea, soups or stews will support immunity and add *agni*. Sweet and versatile cinnamon serves a nervy vata well, keeping blood sugar levels stable and promoting a sense of wellbeing.

Ginger will create the warmth and fire a vata needs to avoid the stress and constipation associated with an excess of coolness. Sipping ginger tea throughout the day will regulate digestion by promoting regular bowel movements. Ginger has also been shown to lower blood triglyceride (fat) levels and ease inflammation throughout the body.

Lemon juice can cleanse the digestive system, helping a stressed and unbalanced vata. A squeeze of zingy lemon in a glass of water each morning or added to salad dressings will stimulate the digestive tract and boost the immune system. Lemon water also helps alkalize the blood, and assists in the maintenance of a healthy weight by supporting the liver and digestive system to do their detoxification jobs efficiently.

Mild spices such as cardamom and cumin are very beneficial, as they warm up vata's cooler tendencies, soothing digestive challenges, maintaining heat and keeping the body grounded. Hotter spices such as cayenne pepper should be avoided, as they can overstimulate the metabolism and cause digestive issues for a vata's sensitive constitution.

Three pitta medicine-chest must-haves

People who fall into the pitta dosha category are renowned for their fiery, strong digestive systems, but too much of that heat can cause imbalance, the effects of which include excessive hunger (leading to overeating and weight gain), the accumulation of toxins, bacterial infections, heartburn and diarrhea. Pittas therefore require a cooling diet to counteract the consequences of excessive fire. Fennel, compared to other herbs, is highly cooling and can soothe digestion, resulting in a more adequate uptake of nutrients and lowered gut inflammation. Coconut oil would be the best cooking oil; it's not only highly satiating but also supports the levels of good bacteria in the gut necessary for stable digestion and immunity against infections. Garnishing with mint is known to reduce a raging appetite by curbing cravings while providing the cooling balance a fiery pitta needs.

Another cooling culinary staple is pineapple, a balancing food for pittas, but only if it's ripe and sweet. Pittas – who require sweetness to balance their sharp, penetrating, sour nature – should avoid underripe sour fruits. The bromelain enzyme in pineapple is highly anti-inflammatory, with blood-thinning effects, helping to prevent weight-related illnesses such as stroke and heart disease.

Coconuts are sweet, smooth and cooling, perfect for a fiery pitta. For pittas who are out of balance in the weight department, coconuts offer insulin-stabilizing effects, preventing overeating and excessive appetite.

Mint pacifies the pitta dosha through its highly cooling effects on the digestive system. Mint has been used throughout history to treat a range of gastrointestinal disorders, and when eaten regularly can help calm a pitta's overactive appetite.

Three kapha medicine-chest must-haves

Kaphas display imbalance through mental and physical stagnation, and are the most prone to excessive weight gain. If you fall into the kapha crew, you'll require some extra stimulation through your food, so your best options are fiery spices such as cayenne pepper, which is known for speeding up the metabolism and burning fat. When imbalanced, kaphas will also show signs of water retention, sluggish bowels and low energy. Artichokes are a wonderful food for promoting healthy bowels by providing the prebiotics required for good bacteria in the digestive tract. Scattering cilantro on your meals or cooking with ground coriander seeds will act as a natural diuretic, reducing water retention and stimulating digestive processes.

Cayenne pepper's fiery spiciness is exactly what tired kaphas require to boost their circulation, increase their energy and kick-start their metabolism. Cayenne pepper is also well known for its weight-reducing properties, helping to decrease calorie intake, shrinking fat tissue and lowering fat levels in the blood.

Studies have linked eating artichokes with a decrease in fatigue. Kaphas need all the help they can get in this department, since fatigue prevents the use of energy for healthy levels of movement. Artichokes are also metabolism-boosting and high in fiber, helping the bowels get moving and eliminating the build-up of fat and toxins.

Cilantro is highly detoxifying, and this is just what a kapha's lagging digestive system requires. Did you know that much of the weight gain people experience is not actually fat, but mucus the body produces to surround the toxins and protect itself? Thankfully, cilantro draws these toxins out of the digestive tract, minimizing this unnecessary weight gain.

Eating with the seasons

Have you ever noticed that you thrive in a particular climate? Do certain seasons leave you craving certain types, textures and temperatures of food? When the weather changes, do you find your mood darkening? If so, read on . . .

We each have an instinct that drives us toward particular eating and lifestyle behaviors that will pacify or balance our dosha so that we can achieve thriving health. By tuning in to that instinct and further understanding the way your own dosha reacts to the changing weather, you can apply the wisdom of Ayurvedic eating principles to ensure you maintain a sense of balance and vitality throughout the highs and lows of the seasons. The recipes in this book are arranged by season, and I have included seasonal meal planners for each dosha on the following pages.

SPRING AND SUMMER

Late spring and summer mirror the qualities of the pitta dosha. If you're a pitta, this season is likely to unbalance you and knock you around, leading to stress, anger, irritability, acne, heartburn, acid reflux and weight gain. If your dominant pitta needs pacifying, focus on cooling and sweet foods such as cucumbers, watermelon, salads and fruit smoothies instead of heavy, cooked foods that will fire you up.

A wonderful drink to indulge in is my Chill Your Pitta Rose Petal Tea (page 127).

Vatas embrace the heat and humidity of the warmer months to soothe their tendencies toward skin dryness, anxiety and hyperactivity. If you're a vata, sweet and sour fruits and salty foods will enable you to flourish during these seasons – try the Blueberry and Lavender Smoothie (page 128). Both cooked and raw foods will provide balance if your digestion is strong, but you should avoid too many salads and light, airy foods.

If kapha is your dominant dosha, you'll need to pay special attention to your diet during periods of high humidity in summer, as these will intensify your already heavy, watery nature. Summer for kaphas is a breeding ground for lethargy, depression and sluggishness. To combat this, you'll need to focus more on drier, crunchier foods that have pungent, astringent and bitter flavors. These include apples, berries, lemons and limes, along with crunchy vegetables such as fennel and asparagus, but keep sauces or oily dressings to a minimum. You'll love my Cumin Scrambled Eggs and Greens (page 98).

AUTUMN

Autumn is the season of vata. Vatas tend to have energy of movement, dryness, coolness and lightness. To please your vata, consume an abundance of warmer cooked foods that are easy to digest. Balancing and grounding foods include root vegetables, such as potatoes and rutabagas, and slow-cooked meats, activated nuts and seeds, lentils, rice and denser fruits. Avoid too many light, raw and cool fruits and vegetables.

Fiery pittas are naturally pacified by the light airiness of autumn. To maintain your tightrope-walking balance, avoid overindulging in cooked foods and in grounding root vegetables. If you do eat them occasionally, they should be warm rather than hot, and always accompanied by a green salad with such ingredients as leafy greens, raw broccoli, green beans and fresh herbs.

If you're a kapha, you'll benefit from the uplifting cool air of autumn, but you should avoid too many meals with watery textures, such as soups and stews, and eat oils only in moderation. Focus on pungent, spicy, astringent and bitter meals. Woody herbs such as rosemary, thyme and sage are beneficial, as is a focus on vegetables rather than watery fruits. Cauliflower, garlic, spring onions (scallions), kale and kohlrabi are wonderful caretaker vegetables to include in autumn. Bircher Muesli (see page 173) gives a punchy breakfast boost to charge up the kapha engines.

WINTER

Winter brings cool air and often wet weather, which are synonymous with all-round kapha characteristics. Kaphas should be especially mindful and set an intention to pacify their dosha in order to maintain stability and avoid depression, weight gain and lethargy. Now is the time to increase your digestive fire by eating spicier and more bitter foods that are lighter, airier and warmer. Lighten up your day with a cup of Weight-reducing Lemon Tea (page 204). Homemade granola with quinoa, buckwheat, oats, cinnamon and ginger will increase your fire in the morning and rev you up for the day. Fall in love with lightweight curries infused with turmeric, black pepper, fennel and paprika.

Pitta is typically hot, oily, smooth and light, the opposite of winter. While the coolness of winter will be very balancing, excessive rain may leave pittas feeling stressed and out of control. Counteract this by eating cooling, dry, heavy foods such as basmati rice, chickpea (garbanzo bean), lentil and chicken breast dishes. A Cilantro and Mint Lassi (page 205) will fill you and chill you at the same time.

Fickle vatas will be aggravated by the cold winter weather, leading to sensitive digestion, a weak immune system and restlessness. Now is the time to load up on grounding root vegetables and meals that are sweet, heavy, steadfast and warm. Root vegetable soups and stews or stewed fruits with warming cardamom and cloves are wonderfully grounding. Ginger tea will add balancing fire and aid digestion.

Eat your biggest meal in the middle of the day and try not to eat sweet foods in the evening. In India I learned that in traditional Ayurvedic eating, sweets should not be eaten last, as the sugars can increase blood sugar levels, resulting in the pancreas having to perform extra work and possibly becoming overloaded. By increasing nutrient-rich foods on your non-fasting days, you'll keep your metabolism boosted and your appetite in check. You'll also supercharge your body for all-day energy.

SEASONAL MEAL PLANNERS

On the following pages, I've mapped out meal plans that include two fasting days per week to fast-track cleansing and optimize digestion. Use them as a guide, and feel free to swap my suggestions with other dishes you enjoy. Note that the numbers in brackets indicate the pages where the recipes appear.

MEAL PLANNER FOR VATA IN SPRING/SUMMER

	Breakfast	Mid-morning	Afternoon tea	Main meal	Light meal
Monday (fasting day)	Orange Cinnamon Porridge (248)	Saffron Lemonade (127)	Small bowl of Kitchari (261)	Fasting	Microherb Omelette (96)
Tuesday	Microherb Omelette (96)	Digestive Lassi (93)	Oven-baked Saffron Chicken with Lime (113)	Halva (121)	Green Bean Subji (136)
Wednesday	Cup of Life Morning Broth (91)	Banana, Raspberry and Flax Breakfast Whip (129)	Spicy Lamb Koftas (117)	Pistachio Truffles (121)	Brown Rice Nori (102)
Thursday (fasting day)	Warm water	Blueberry and Lavender Smoothie (128)	Lemongrass Chicken with Grilled Asparagus (249)	Fasting	Green Bean, Radish and Avocado Salad (248)
Friday	Stewed Fruits with Cashew Cream (97)	Saffron Lemonade (127)	Baked Fish with Flaxseed Crust (152)	Saffron and Coconut Tapioca Pudding (160)	Saffron and Squash Soup (146)
Saturday	Summer Breakfast Parfait (130)	Summer Smoothie (129)	Green Pea Curry (155)	Pistachio Truffles (121)	Carrot, Mango, Arugula and Sunflower Salad with Orange Dressing (101)
Sunday	Pistachio and Blueberry Pancakes (133)	Digestive Lassi (93)	Crumbed Fish with Sautéed Beans (156)	Aloe Vera Jelly (157)	Anti-inflammatory Spring Pea Soup (111)

MEAL PLANNER FOR VATA IN AUTUMN/WINTER

	Breakfast	Mid-morning	Afternoon tea	Main meal	Light meal
Monday (fasting day)	Turmeric, Cardamom and Cumin Tea (204)	Cup of Life Morning Broth (91)	Small bowl of Kitchari (261)	Fasting	Double-dosha-pacifying Soup (186)
Tuesday	Spiced Amaranth (206)	Vata-calming Fig and Almond Butter Whip (168)	Slow-cooked Balancing Vegetables (191)	Lemon-infused Cardamom Biscuits (229)	Squash Bake (218)
Wednesday	Avocado and Goat's Cheese on Carrot and Zucchini Loaf (174)	Weight-reducing Lemon Tea (204)	Carrot and Ginger Soup (219)	Vata-calming Fig and Almond Butter Whip (168)	Coconut Brown Rice with Ginger and Black Sesame Seeds (216)
Thursday (fasting day)	Warm water + Orange Cinnamon Porridge (248)	Fasting	Lemongrass Chicken with Grilled Asparagus (249)	Fasting	Small bowl of Kitchari (261)
Friday	Indian Spiced Vegetable Porridge (209)	Turmeric, Cardamom and Cumin Tea (204)	Tuna Tikka Curry (226)	Chocolate Fudge (195)	Sweet Potato Hash (180) + Spinach Pancake (170)
Saturday	Spinach Pancakes (170)	Holy Basil Coffee (167)	Quinoa Pilau (222)	Chai Crème Brûlée (231)	Vegetable Thoran (182)
Sunday	Fig, Cardamom and Quinoa Bowl (173)	Almond Milk Chai with Turmeric and Fennel (203)	Traditional Lamb Korma (192)	Stewed Apple with Cloves (196)	Goat's Cheese, Fennel and Walnut Salad (211)

MEAL PLANNER FOR PITTA IN SPRING/SUMMER

	Breakfast	Mid-morning	Afternoon tea	Main meal	Light meal
Monday (fasting day)	Warm water + Egg-white Omelette with Zucchini and Mushrooms (252)	Fasting	Small bowl of Kitchari (261)	Fasting	Cassava Chips (144) + Carrot and Beet Raita (235)
Tuesday	Pitta-pacifying Oatmeal with Summer Fruits (135)	Chill Your Pitta Rose Petal Tea (127)	Oven-baked Saffron Chicken with Lime (113)	Aloe Vera Jelly (157)	Green Bean Subji (136)
Wednesday	Summer Breakfast Parfait (130)	Brazil Nut, Dandelion and Cardamom Latte (90)	Crumbed Fish with Sautéed Beans (156)	Coconut Bark with Rosewater, Pistachios and Raspberries (158)	Cream of Arugula Soup (112)
Thursday (fasting day)	Warm water	Cup of Life Morning Broth (91)	Grilled Lemon Shrimp with Cauliflower Mash (253)	Fasting	Small bowl of Kitchari (261)
Friday	Summer Breakfast Parfait (130)	Chill Your Pitta Rose Petal Tea (127)	Tea-poached Chicken with Green Beans (151)	Minted Strawberry Slushie (93)	Calming Cucumber and Coconut Soup (148)
Saturday	Cup of Life Morning Broth (91)	Banana, Raspberry and Flax Breakfast Whip (129)	Baked Fish with Flaxseed Crust (152)	Coconut Bark with Rosewater, Pistachios and Raspberries (158)	Liver-cleansing Green Dip (106) + Om Pudi (244) or Oats Upma (109)
Sunday	Oven-baked Peach and Berry Pancake (94)	Brazil Nut, Dandelion and Cardamom Latte (90)	Spiced Basmati Pilau (245)	Saffron and Coconut Tapioca Pudding (160)	Anti-inflammatory Spring Pea Soup (111)

MEAL PLANNER FOR PITTA IN AUTUMN/WINTER

	Breakfast	Mid-morning	Afternoon tea	Main meal	Light meal
Monday (fasting day)	Warm water	Cup of Life Morning Broth (91)	Small bowl of Kitchari (261)	Fasting	Egg-white Omelette with Zucchini and Mushrooms (252)
Tuesday	Bircher Muesli (173)	Cilantro and Mint Lassi (205)	Slow-cooked Balancing Vegetables (191)	Pomegranate and Lime Cheesecake (197)	Turmeric Cauliflower and Peas (178)
Wednesday	Indian Spiced Vegetable Porridge (209)	Pitta Beauty Brew (203)	Butternut Squash Curry (187)	Stewed Apple with Cloves (196)	Vegetable Thoran (182)
Thursday (fasting day)	Warm water	Egg-white Omelette with Zucchini and Mushrooms (252)	Small bowl of Kitchari (261)	Fasting	Grilled Lemon Shrimp with Cauliflower Mash (253)
Friday	Fig, Cardamom and Quinoa Bowl (173)	Holy Basil Coffee (167)	Quinoa Pilau (222)	Lemon-infused Cardamom Biscuits (229)	Immune-boosting Soup (221)
Saturday	Cup of Life Morning Broth (91)	Pitta Beauty Brew (203)	Tuna Tikka Curry (226)	Chai Crème Brûlée (231)	Baked Squash, Quinoa and Kale (215)
Sunday	Bircher Muesli (173)	Lime, Mint and Carrot Zinger (168)	One-pot Lamb and Swiss Chard (225)	Lemony Coconut Mousse (232)	Creamy Mushroom Soup (183)

MEAL PLANNER FOR KAPHA IN SPRING/SUMMER

	Breakfast	Mid-morning	Afternoon tea	Main meal	Light meal
Monday (fasting day)	Warm water + Baked Apple with Prunes, Cinnamon and Cardamom (256)	Cup of Life Morning Broth (91)	Fasting	Spinach and Shrimp Curry (257)	Watercress, Fennel and Ruby Grapefruit Salad (108)
Tuesday	Cumin Scrambled Eggs and Greens (98)	Saffron Lemonade (127)	Aloe Vera Jelly (157)	Energizing Vegetable Stew (149)	Asparagus with Mustard and Tarragon (105) + handful of Spiced Pecans (139)
Wednesday	Digestion Soup (145)	Kapha-balancing Tea (91)	Digestive Lassi (93)	Indian Infused Chicken (114)	Eggplant Bharta (140)
Thursday (fasting day)	Cup of Life Morning Broth (91)	Mushroom, Broccoli and Sunflower Seed Quinoa Pilau (256)	Fasting	Small bowl of Kitchari (261)	Fasting
Friday	Banana and Buckwheat Hotcakes (134)	Saffron Lemonade (127)	Kapha-balancing Tea (91)	Green Pea Curry (155)	Baby Spinach, Pine Nut and Pomegranate Salad (107)
Saturday	Cumin Scrambled Eggs and Greens (98)	Digestive Lassi (93)	Handful of Spiced Pecans (139)	Anti-inflammatory Spring Pea Soup (111)	Daikon and Endive Salad (143)
Sunday	Minted Strawberry Slushie (93)	Cup of Life Morning Broth (91)	Kapha-balancing Tea (91)	Crumbed Fish with Sautéed Beans (156)	Cream of Arugula Soup (112)

MEAL PLANNER FOR KAPHA IN AUTUMN/WINTER

	Breakfast	Mid-morning	Afternoon tea	Main meal	Light meal
Monday (fasting day)	Cup of Life Morning Broth (91)	Kapha-balancing Tea (91)	Fasting	Mushroom, Broccoli and Sunflower Seed Quinoa Pilau (256)	Fasting
Tuesday	Weight-reducing Lemon Tea (204)	Turmeric, Cardamom and Cumin Tea (204)	Raw Cacao Smoothie (169)	Tuna Tikka Curry (226)	Apple, Celery and Spiced Pecan Salad (179)
Wednesday	Bircher Muesli (173)	Cilantro and Mint Lassi (205)	Stewed Apple with Cloves (196)	One-pot Lamb and Swiss Chard (225)	Replenishing Red Lentil Soup (185)
Thursday (fasting day)	Warm water + Baked Apple with Prunes, Cinnamon and Cardamom (256)	Holy Basil Coffee (167)	Fasting	Spinach and Shrimp Curry (257)	Ayurvedic Weight-loss Soup (221)
Friday	Weight-reducing Lemon Tea (204) + Spiced Amaranth (206)	Turmeric, Cardamom and Cumin Tea (204)	Spiced Poached Pears with Orange (231)	Fragrant Fish Stew (188)	Baked Squash, Quinoa and Kale (215)
Saturday	Breakfast Borscht (208)	Holy Basil Coffee (167)	Stewed Apple with Cloves (196)	Mung Bean Dhal (228)	Creamy Mushroom Soup (183)
Sunday	Weight-reducing Lemon Tea (204) + Spinach Pancakes (170)	Raw Cacao Smoothie (169)	Spiced Amaranth (206)	Butternut Squash Curry (187)	Cumin Creamed Spinach (212) + Indian Dosas (240) *or* Brown Rice Crepes (243)

Mindful eating

Have you ever noticed that when your emotions are out of balance, you can lose or gain weight in what seems like the blink of an eye? There's no doubt that the mind and body are intrinsically linked, and current nutritional research is revealing an intricate connection between your emotional state and the foods you choose to eat. By eating mindfully, according to your individual needs, you have every chance of avoiding unnecessary weight gain and reaching your wellness potential while maintaining a stable mood.

Given so many people are suffering from some form of digestive disturbance, it's important to look at our unique mind–body connection, as well as when we eat, where we eat, how we eat, why we eat and what season we're in. This foundation of Ayurvedic nutrition encourages a conscious way of living. It's a way of embracing food as the energy force it is, and of understanding how our own unique nature – our dosha – and the influences around us determine how well our food will serve us. Ayurveda grounds itself in the fact that our dietary needs and our digestion are affected by the rhythms of nature and the changes that occur in our life. More generally, it asks that we eat food mindfully and with gratitude, and that this food be fresh, of the highest quality, digestible, delicious, lovingly prepared and satisfying to all our senses.

How many times have you eaten a meal while doing something else? Think of those mornings when you've been late for work and you've eaten on the run, or had a quick nibble as you worked at your desk on your computer. We're so used to being constantly on the go, but we can become riddled with stress, which makes it even harder to prioritize taking time out to enjoy and appreciate a meal. Regularly eating on the run will set you up

for failure. For optimal health and energy, we need to respect and nurture our gut, and in particular our digestion. At a practical level, it means taking time to really honor our food – from selecting it to preparing it and finally eating it.

Mindfulness is centered on bringing your full attention to yourself and what's happening in the present moment. Mindful eating is therefore a practice of engaging with food in a way that takes into account the present moment, *where* you are, *who* you are, *why* you're doing it and *how* it's happening. Think about taking notice of the color, texture, aroma and flavor of your food. Sit down in a comfortable space with your food and savor each mouthful lovingly. Be mindful of where it came from, enjoy the different colors on your plate, actually feel the different textures in your mouth and on your palate, smell your food and, if you can, enjoy it with your friends in a relaxing environment.

Furthering your mindful eating practice can involve stopping and contemplating the origins of your food, being present and mentally focused during a meal, spending time creatively preparing your food, engaging and being aware of all of your senses, practicing thankfulness, and eating only when you're truly hungry. Never eat standing up or when distracted, and avoid the temptation to multitask. All of these things will help you control your appetite so that you can choose the amount and type of food you need to maintain a healthy weight and eat right for your shape.

MINDFUL EATING EVERY DAY

Here are five practical ways to incorporate mindfulness into your daily eating habits.

1 Make friends with food

Sometimes it can be hard to practice self-control when you're being constantly bombarded with unhealthy food choices throughout the day, from advertising, marketing or even pressure from others. It will help you to eat right for your shape if you come to understand your body's biological needs and then make a commitment to supporting those needs through healthy, nourishing, clean foods. By doing this, you can arrive at a place where you're at peace with your plate and can fill your body with foods that bring you nourishment and healing.

2 Draw your awareness inward

If you have a tendency to overeat, then practicing discipline with your meals and self-restraint when it comes to portion size will help you develop mindfulness of what you're putting into your body, and a fundamental self-respect. Remember to listen to your inner voice when eating. If you still have food left on your plate but you're not hungry, don't force yourself to eat it. Be aware of your body if it's telling you you've had enough. Almost immediately, you'll start to notice the role your emotions play in your eating habits and how you can control those emotions while still satisfying your biological needs.

3 Eat when you're hungry

One reason our weight can sometimes spiral out of control is that, somewhere along the line, we've stopped listening to our body signals that naturally tell us when we're hungry. Learning how to identify true hunger and tuning in to that hunger attentively is a way to cultivate a genuinely healthy appetite while still maintaining mindfulness. There are so many distractions that lead us away from our natural way of eating and convince us we're hungry. If you're unclear whether you're hungry or not, do something else instead until you *do* feel hungry, then check in with your inner wisdom to see how you feel afterward.

4 Use swaps to satisfy cravings

Cravings can disrupt our efforts to have a healthy relationship with food. In Ayurvedic philosophy, there are two types of cravings: a biological need and a psychological desire. A biological need is one that satisfies a certain hunger you may have for something sweet or sour, while a psychological desire makes you crave junk food or chocolate cake. In this instance, instead of satisfying your psychological desire, feed the craving without depriving yourself by finding a healthy alternative for a particular food. If, for example, you feel like chocolate cake, don't judge yourself harshly for wanting it, but indulge instead in a dessert from this book. That way, you can satisfy your urges while still maintaining your shape.

5 Identify emotional triggers

Psychological desires can also be caused by emotions that may be missing in your life. If, for example, you get home from work and you're on your own, you may be craving a hug, but instead you reach into the fridge and eat something unhealthy. This is what we call comfort eating. Because it makes you eat at night and when you're not hungry, it's a fast track to weight gain. If you use mindfulness in this situation, it will help you stop your emotional eating and understand that you're craving food in response to a certain missing emotion.

Eliminating toxins

As we get older it can become harder to lose weight, even through a strict exercise and diet program. Ayurveda uses age-old techniques that target weight loss by igniting digestive fire (*agni*) and reducing the accumulation of toxins within your body, promoting optimum digestion. *Ama* (toxins) can be the result of an unhealthy diet, chronic stress and environmental contaminants. There are two types of toxin: water-based and fat-based. The water-based toxins can be eliminated from your body through nutrition and exercise; the fat-based toxins – which lead to weight gain, particularly around the midsection, stomach and thighs – can be eliminated by cleansing the body through daily practices such as baths with Epsom salts, oil pulling, warm oil massages, yoga poses (see page 61) and detoxification.

Massage the body with warm oil to improve circulation, activate the lymphatic system, and aid in detoxification. If you have access to a steam bath, this will support your body's natural self-cleansing functions.

Epsom salts, lavender and baking soda bath
Try to take a detox bath at least twice a week. When you have a bath with Epsom salts, the magnesium sulfate is absorbed through the skin and draws toxins from the body. It also sedates the nervous system to relax you completely, reduces swelling, loosens muscles, relieves muscular aches and pains, and is even a natural emollient and exfoliator. Baking soda alkalizes the body and helps eliminate acidic waste.

Add to a warm bath while the water is running: 2 cups (3 lb/1.3 kg) Epsom salts, 1 cup (1 lb 4 oz/550 g) bicarbonate of soda (baking soda) and 2 drops lavender essential oil. Once the bath is at the right level and temperature for you, climb in slowly and let your body soak for 20 minutes. Avoid having a detox bath if you're pregnant, dehydrated, have heart problems, or have open wounds.

If you don't have time for a full bath, enjoy a foot bath instead!

Oil pulling
Here's a simple introductory technique to try each morning. Place 1 tablespoon (20 ml) extra virgin cold-pressed coconut oil in your mouth upon rising, before you've eaten or drunk anything. Swish the oil around your mouth for 10–20 minutes, then spit it out. Never swallow the oil, which will be full of bacteria. Brush your teeth and tongue thoroughly afterward, to remove any excess oil. It's best to buy a specific toothbrush for using after oil pulling, and wash it thoroughly using 3 percent hydrogen peroxide solution to prevent the build-up of bad bacteria.

Turbocharging weight loss

Now for the exciting part! I'm going to guide you gently toward turbocharging your weight loss. One of the biggest factors in weight gain is stress, which is why it's essential to keep your stress levels to a minimum. If you feel that stress is becoming a problem for you and hindering all your weight-loss efforts, why not have a shot at the yoga poses and breathing exercises starting on page 63?

Ayurveda is not a fad diet; it's been road-tested for more than 5000 years and allows you as an individual to follow the rhythms of nature, the seasons and your body. To kick-start your weight loss, I'm going to ask you to consider intermittent fasting as an ongoing practice to implement twice a week.

If you've read my previous book, *Heal Your Gut*, you're probably already aware that I'm all about gut health. One of the most important steps in my personal recovery was healing my digestive system. As my gut lining started to repair itself and my gut flora became balanced, many aspects of my health dramatically improved. It's fascinating what an astoundingly accurate reflection of our emotional state our gut is. Conversely, if we take care of our digestive system, our emotions and mood will be affected in a positive way and our weight will return to normal.

Ayurveda reached the same conclusion many years ago with its recommendation that each meal should consist only of the amount of food you can hold in your cupped hands. Think about eating enough to feel satisfied but not full or bloated. If you overeat and your stomach is bursting, your *agni*

(digestive fire), stomach acids and enzymes cannot perform their duties. Overeating means that partially digested food hangs around in your digestive system and can become toxic. *Ama*, a toxic by-product of incomplete digestion and the root cause of many human diseases, will then be present in your body.

INTERMITTENT FASTING (IF)

To begin eating right for your shape, your digestive system will periodically need a little rest in order to function and perform at its best. That's when IF can be really helpful. Twice a week, I follow IF to give my digestive system some well-needed restorative time. IF doesn't mean you have to stop eating altogether and starve yourself for the entire day. It simply means eating less and focusing on easily digestible foods that are akin to your dosha.

IF provides a long list of benefits; clinical studies have shown that it can reduce blood triglycerides (fats), LDL (bad) cholesterol, blood pressure, inflammation and free-radical damage. It also helps promote cell repair and switches on fat-burning, increasing levels of the human growth hormone, which in turn promotes muscle growth and boosts fat loss. When you fast for a period of time, your metabolic rate is increased, making you a more efficient fat-burning machine. IF also helps lower blood glucose, normalize insulin and leptin sensitivity, and normalize ghrelin (the hunger hormone) for better appetite control.

AYURVEDIC FASTING

There are many IF protocols you can discover and each is different. Ayurvedic practice leans toward eating three meals a day with no snacking, and eating your lightest meal at the end of the day and as early as possible. Ayurvedic IF involves consuming 500 calories (2000 kilojoules) during the day so that you can switch to fat-burning mode.

In Ayurvedic nutrition, the ancient practice of fasting on Kitchari (page 261) – also known as partaking in a kitchari cleanse – is considered to be a fantastic cleansing ritual. Kitchari, a staple comfort food of India, is calming and soothing to the digestive tract and warming to the body. This porridge-like soup is made using a traditional mix of rice and mung beans (or sometimes another type of bean), with added spices and sometimes vegetables. In kitchari fasting, the body receives a limited range of foods, requiring production of fewer digestive enzymes, leading to easy digestion and cleansing of the body. You can do a kitchari cleanse at any time between IF to further detoxify your body.

Most Ayurveda-derived kitchari recipes use basmati rice as the primary ingredient, as it is considered suitable for all three constitutional types. Soaking the rice and beans first is recommended.

FASTING TIPS

If you're wondering when to fast, pick two non-consecutive days. I fast on Mondays and Thursdays but you should choose days that work with your lifestyle – take a look at the meal planners starting on page 46 for inspiration. I believe in the metabolism-boosting properties of a healthy meal during the period of highest digestion, so I eat my largest meal at lunchtime. On my IF days, I try to eat dinner as early as possible to achieve double benefits, and I eat small quantities of nutrient-rich, easy-to-digest, seasonal foods suited to my dosha during the "feeding" phase. This lightens the load on my gut and prepares my body for a longer overnight "fasting" phase than usual, to give my digestive system twelve to sixteen hours of complete rest.

As with everything else, better results come with consistency and working within your own body's needs. You'll experience cravings when you first begin fasting, and this is natural. Don't be tempted to snack, but instead try to feel positive about being hungry. It's a very good sign that your *agni* is becoming stronger. Because it's no longer busy digesting food, your *agni* will begin the job of cleansing any toxic backlog of *ama* in your body.

I've created some special fasting recipes (see page 247) and you can also keep an eye out in the other recipes for the fasting (scales) icon.

Incorporating IF into your life two days a week can be a smooth transition, and I've come up with six tips to get you started.

1 Choose your foods carefully

During IF, try to focus on seasonal produce, healthy protein and good fats such as eggs, avocado and fish. Minimize carbs such as grains, bread and potatoes.

2 Stay hydrated

On waking, drink warm water to help flush out and evacuate your bowel. Staying well hydrated will make the fasting periods much easier to get through. Sipping warm water between meals aids digestion, helps remove any build-up of toxic *ama*, and can reduce the compulsion to snack.

3 Change your thoughts

Think of fasting as a self-care practice, an essential timeout for your gut for which your body and health will thank you. This is not another fad diet or period of deprivation, and you're working within your own constitution and bodily systems.

4 Keep busy

Plan your IF for days when you know you won't be home and tempted to reach for an unhealthy snack.

5 Do some form of gentle exercise

Try the yoga poses starting on page 63. Regular physical activity will help you achieve even better results. Practicing yoga is like giving a wonderful massage to your internal organs to create harmony. Yoga can reshape your body by providing total body conditioning plus mental clarity and strength. A good time for yoga is at sunrise or whenever you first rise. I've noted which dosha will find each pose particularly balancing, but try them all to improve your digestion and fat-burning capabilities.

6 Remember to start slowly

Maybe start with only one day a week, then work your way up to two days a week. If your goal is weight loss, two or three days will yield optimum results. Once you get used to it, you won't feel hungry any more, and you'll be amazed how focused, clear and energetic you are.

The golden rules for weight loss

As you embark on your quest to lose weight, it can be overwhelming at times. Remember these three golden rules and you'll be on the right track.

1 Indulge in real food

To experience the freedom of optimum health, it's important to follow the art of eating wisely. Because Ayurveda is a nature-based approach, eating real food is the key. It might seem very basic, but sometimes it can be difficult to find real food that has been grown without the use of pesticides and chemicals. Trying to find foods that are fresh and as close to their natural state as possible is fundamental to your health. Look for locally grown and in-season produce, and try to avoid leftovers, which are unbalancing to the doshas because food loses its vital energy after a night in the fridge and can become slimy and heavy. (If you would like to eat leftovers, ensure that you reheat them with ghee and black pepper.) Nature gives us the nourishment we need. When you start to eat real food, you'll be surprised at how quickly your body will respond, especially when reaching your weight-loss goals.

2 Eat your biggest meal in the middle of the day

When you do this, your liver will be less congested and overloaded when you go to bed, so that you can enjoy a restful and healing sleep. The body's metabolic rate picks up between 10 am and 2 pm, and your digestion will be at its most powerful during that time. Eating a large meal at the end of the day will overwork your liver and you'll wake up tired and lacking in energy. Eating your lighter final meal of the day before sunset will enable you to lose weight, as you'll be giving your body space and time to process and assimilate the food. It will also give your body permission to burn fat. Remember not to drink too much water during meals, as it dilutes the gastric juices. Many of the Ayurvedic practitioners I met in India recommended filling half your stomach with solid food, a quarter with liquids, and leaving a quarter empty. In other words, try to eat only until you're three-quarters full.

3 Stop trying to be perfect, already!

When you stop trying to be perfect, you can relax. Even if you're one of those over-achievers who got top marks at school, it may have come at a price, and perhaps you still push yourself too hard or demand a lot from yourself. Being perfect all the time can lead to disordered eating habits. Have you ever in the past put food into the good and bad basket? This perfectionism and extreme attention to detail will not bring harmony to your life but will only make you feel bad about yourself in the long run. Remember, it's good to eat clean, but not "squeaky clean." I encourage you to enjoy real, whole, natural foods most of the time, by following the 80/20 rule (see below). Make time for your meals and really relax and enjoy your food – it's there to nourish your body. If you make your meals the fun part of the day and start giving them a bit more attention and gratitude, you'll naturally lean toward eating more healthily and not reaching for the nearest convenience food.

The 80/20 rule

This philosophy will ensure you stay healthy but continue to enjoy life without ever feeling deprived. Eating well 80 percent of the time and indulging in whatever you enjoy the other 20 percent of the time ensures an "everything in moderation" approach, keeping your body on an even keel so that you'll never feel tempted into disordered thinking or eating.

PART 2

Yoga and breathing exercises

Yoga poses

Imagine a tree with two branches, each unique, with its own characteristics, but both originating from the same place and sharing a common history and foundation. That's a good way of looking at how Ayurveda and yoga are interrelated and entwined.

Yoga practice has direct links to an Ayurvedic lifestyle, and yoga poses have an intrinsic vata, pitta, and kapha nature. Practicing the poses for your dosha on the following pages will help you keep your body healthy, your dosha balanced and your mind focused and positive.

If you have a vata constitution, you can balance your dosha by practicing yoga poses that add the qualities of warmth, stability, grounding and focus. Vatas should practice at a slow, steady pace and focus on the foundation of the pose to achieve stability. Hold the postures for a short time, then repeat them a few times.

For pitta, your yoga practice should be cooling, encourage compassion and acceptance and not be rushed. The poses should be practiced with a light-hearted attitude, in a cool room that allows for freedom and movement. Avoid judging yourself or becoming overly critical, and remember to let go.

For kapha, your yoga practice should create space, lightness, stimulation, warmth and buoyancy. Challenge yourself by using a strong and forceful breath and, just as you are about to release the pose, take one more breath in and out through the nose, expanding your body and feeling the energy and lightness fuel you.

Cat–cow pose (*vidalasana*) **Ⓥ**

Loosens the spine while releasing head, neck, shoulders and pelvic tension; also centers, relaxes and stills the mind and creates a sense of tranquillity.

1. Start on your hands and knees.

2. Inhale, drawing your tailbone toward the floor and your navel towards the ceiling, arching your spine. In the same movement, bring your chin toward your chest to lengthen the back of your neck.

3. Exhale, bringing your tailbone back up and pushing down with your belly and chest, making your spine concave. In the same movement, extend your chin slightly up and out, opening your throat. Repeat steps 2 and 3 for five breaths, allowing your breath to guide you.

Standing forward bend pose
(*uttanasana*)

Increases flexibility in the hamstrings and spine, calms and cools the mind, improves digestion, relieves digestive problems such as constipation, slows the heart and nourishes the brain cells.

1. Start from a standing pose with your big toes touching, heels slightly apart, tailbone tucked under and your arms alongside you with your palms facing forward.

2. Inhale and sweep your arms out to the sides, then up above your head.

3. Exhale and gradually bend forward from your hips, lengthening your spine and lowering your upper body over your legs.

4. Relax your upper body and bring your left hand to your right elbow and your right hand to your left elbow. (If you feel any discomfort behind your knees or in your hamstrings, feel free to bend your knees.)

5. Hold for ten breaths then release slowly, rolling up your spine one vertebra at a time.

Warrior II pose (*virabhadrasana* II) Ⓚ

Strengthens the legs, back, shoulders and arms, building stamina, opens the hips and chest, and improves balance; its name refers to the fierce warrior, an incarnation of Shiva.

1. Start in a standing position, then jump (if that's comfortable) or step out so your feet are about 4 feet (120 centimetres) apart.

2. Inhale and pull back your shoulders to open your chest, stretching your arms out from your shoulders to the sides, with your palms facing the floor.

3. In the same movement, turn your left foot 90 degrees to the left, aligning your left heel with your right heel.

4. Exhale and bend your left knee, with your knee directly over your ankle. Hold this position for 30–60 seconds and feel the line of energy running from the tips of your left fingers to the tips of your right fingers. Inhale and slowly straighten your left knee, then repeat on the other side.

Triangle pose (*trikonasana*) Ⓥ Ⓟ

Improves digestion and alleviates constipation.

1. From a standing pose, step out so your feet are moderately widely spaced.

2. Turn your left foot out by 90 degrees and your right foot in slightly.

3. Inhale and, keeping your legs straight, reach out to the sides with your arms while tensing your right thigh.

4. Exhale and drop your left hand down to the side of your left shin or ankle or to the floor beside your left foot. Your right hand should be in the air. With your chest open and your shoulders vertically in line, reach toward the ceiling with your right fingers and look up toward them. Hold for five breaths, then return gently to your standing position. Switch sides and repeat.

Supine spinal twist (*supta matsyendrasana*)

Massages the abdominal organs, alleviating digestive ailments.

1. Lie on your back, then lift your knees and place your feet on the floor directly under your knees.

2. Draw your right knee to your chest and extend your left leg on the floor with the toes of both feet pointing slightly toward your head.

3. Drop your right leg over the left side of your body until your right toes are resting on the floor. At the same time, stretch your right arm to the right side and turn your head to the right while keeping your right shoulder on the floor. Hold for five breaths before lifting your right knee back to your chest.

4. Gently return to your starting position, then repeat on the other side.

Camel pose (*ushtrasana*) Ⓟ

Stretches the stomach and intestines, alleviating constipation.

1. Start in a kneeling position with your knees slightly apart, your thighs perpendicular to the floor and the soles of your feet facing the ceiling.

2. Inhale and draw your hands up your sides as you lean back slightly, pushing your chest upward and your hips forward.

3. Exhale and reach your hands back one at a time to grasp your heels. (If you cannot reach your heels when your feet are flat, curl your toes under and rest on the balls of your feet.)

4. Bring your hips forward so that they are almost over your knees while letting your head fall back, opening your throat. Hold for five breaths, then gently return to your kneeling position.

Seated forward bend (*paschimottanasana*)

Improves digestion and waste removal.

1. Sit on the floor with your legs together and in front of you, your hands resting on your knees. Flex your feet and point your toes toward the ceiling.

2. Contract your quadriceps (front thigh) and inhale while lifting both arms straight up toward the ceiling, lengthening your spine.

3. Exhale, and bend forward with your upper body, hinging at the hips, reaching out with your arms and hands to keep a long spine.

4. Relax your upper back and neck and put your head down while grasping your feet, ankles or calves (depending on your flexibility) and pulling gently to deepen the stretch. Rest your chin on or near your chest and hold for ten breaths. Gently return to sitting upright.

Cobra pose (*bhujangasana*) Ⓚ

Stimulates the abdominal organs, improving digestion.

1. Lie on your belly with your feet together and your head in the air, keeping your neck straight.

2. Place your hands under your shoulders and beside your chest, your palms flat on the floor and your fingers spread with the middle finger facing forward.

3. Inhale and push into your hands to lift your upper body off the mat. Keep your pubic bone on the mat and your shoulders back and down, away from your ears.

4. Roll your shoulders back and lift your chest higher, while keeping your hips on the floor and tensing your buttocks. Hold for five breaths, then release gently and return to your original position.

Wind-relieving pose (*apanasana*) Ⓥ

Massages the ascending and descending colon.

1. Lie on your back, then lift your knees and place your feet on the floor directly under your knees.

2. Hug your knees comfortably to your belly. Hold for ten breaths, then return your feet to the floor.

3. Now hug the right knee, with your left knee pointing upward, for ten breaths.

4. Then hug the left knee, with your right knee pointing upward, for ten breaths. Return to your original position.

Child's pose (*balasana*)

Compresses the abdomen and massages the internal organs.

1. Start in a kneeling position, with your buttocks on your heels, your back straight and your hands resting on your knees.

2. Stretch your body down and forward, with your stomach resting on your thighs, your forehead on the floor and your arms stretched forward with your forearms on the floor. Hold for ten breaths then gently return to a kneeling position.

Corpse pose (*savasana*)

The ultimate posture for all healing. As you lie still, you're allowing stress to melt away and literally creating a healing environment for your body. Your blood will start to flow away from your extremities and toward your digestive organs, which will create the ideal environment for digestion, cleansing and healing.

1. Lie on your back with your legs together, with your feet turned outwards and your arms at 30 degrees from your body with your palms facing upward.
2. Close your eyes and become aware of your breath.
3. Relax into the mat for ten breaths.

Revolved crescent lunge
(parivrtta anjaneyasana) Ⓚ

Massages the abdominal muscles and twists the internal organs to help stimulate digestion. Compressing the colon from right to left can really aid digestion. Detoxifying twists can stimulate the movement of the toxins that accumulate in the body and help usher them out.

1. From a standing position, lunge back with your right leg ensuring that both feet are pointing forward, then twist your upper body to the left.
2. Inhale and place your right hand on the outside (left) of your left foot and reach your left arm upward into the air, twisting from your waist. (If you can't get your right hand and shoulder outside your front knee, place your hand on the inside of your foot.)
3. Gaze up at your left hand and hold for five breaths.
4. Inhale as you slowly stand up again, then repeat on the other side.
5. When you've finished, release slowly from the lunge and return to a standing position. Bring your hands into prayer pose in front of your chest, while bending your head down and closing your eyes (if they were open, they would be looking at your hands).
6. Take a long, slow, deep breath into the belly and relax.

Revolved low lunge
(parivrtta sanchalanasana) Ⓚ

Twists but also stretches the front of the thighs and the groin. Often when our hip flexors are tight, they interfere with our internal organ function, including digestion. Stretching the front of the body helps keep things moving in the right direction.

1. From a standing position, lower your right knee to the floor as far behind you as is comfortable, with your left leg bent at a right angle, then reach back with your left hand to catch your right foot as you lift your right heel up toward your buttocks.
2. Hold for five breaths.
3. Release slowly, then repeat with your left foot.
4. Release slowly, then return to a standing position.

Breathing exercises

Practicing deep breathing daily will help you to not only clear your mind and thoughts, but also to gather the courage and determination you need to achieve your weight-loss goals. By incorporating the following deep-breathing exercises into your daily routine, you'll be increasing the oxygen supply to your cells, thus aiding in fat-burning.

When we feel stressed, our body switches to flight or fight mode, causing it to store fat instead of burning it. Deep breathing and conscious relaxation dramatically reduce our levels of cortisol (the stress hormone in our body, which is also involved in fat storage) to offset fat levels. That's why it's good to neutralise stress hormones and increase our 'happy' hormones with breathing exercises. According to Ayurveda, when our bodies are in balance, we desire foods that are good for us. Conversely, if our mind, body and spirit are not synchronized, we lose our connection with our body's inner intelligence, thwarting our weight-loss goals.

You don't need to go to a yoga studio to practice relaxation. These breathing exercises can be done simply at home, in the backyard, at work or even when you're in your car and stuck in a traffic jam. You can always sneak in a few rhythmic and calming deep breaths to dissolve stress and switch off your fat-storage mechanism – before the lights change!

Alternate nostril breathing (*nadi sodhana*)

Your nose is a clever little instrument, directly linked to your brain and nervous system. Indian yogis believe that diseases are linked to disordered nasal breathing. Just by controlling the breath (*pranayama*) through the daily practice of alternate nostril breathing, you can experience many therapeutic benefits, such as improvement in your sleep patterns, a calmer disposition and a clearer mind. Generally, it's unusual for people to breathe equally through both nostrils, and most favor one nostril over the other. The left nostril is cooling and feminine, for calming and nurturing, while the right nostril is heated and masculine, for doing and energy. When you breathe in through your left nostril, you access the right, "feeling" hemisphere of your brain, while the right nostril opens the left, "thinking" hemisphere of your brain. By breathing slowly and steadily from the right to left nostril, you can open the gateway to your entire brain and merge your thinking.

1. Sit comfortably with your spine lengthened and your shoulders relaxed. Relax your face and jaw.
2. Place your left hand on your left knee, with your palm open to the sky or in *chin mudra*, with the thumb and index finger gently touching at their tips. Lower your head and close your eyes.
3. Place the tips of your right index and middle fingers between your eyebrows, with your thumb gently resting on your right nostril and your ring finger gently resting on your left nostril.

4. Press your thumb down on your right nostril and breathe out gently through your left nostril.
5. Take a long, slow, deep breath in through your left nostril, then press the left nostril gently with your right ring finger while removing your right thumb from your right nostril, and exhale through your right nostril.
6. Inhale through your right nostril and exhale through the left. This completes one round. Start by doing three rounds a day, and then add one round a week until you reach seven rounds.

Ujjayi breathing

This deep, resonant breathing technique helps calm the mind and warm the body. *Ujjayi* is a Sanskrit word meaning "to conquer" or "to be victorious," and this technique is often referred to as the victorious breath. When practicing *ujjayi*, you fill your lungs completely and breathe through your nose while slightly contracting your throat.

1. Sit comfortably with your spine lengthened, your shoulders relaxed and your hands in your lap.
2. Inhale slowly through your nose and, with your mouth almost closed and your throat slightly contracted, exhale through your mouth, producing a hissing sound (like Darth Vader). (If you sound like you're snoring you've gone too far!) Keep the position of your throat natural and ensure that the sound originates from your throat rather than your nose.
3. Inhale, producing the same sound, with your throat in the same position.
4. Begin to balance your inhalation with your exhalation and focus on balancing the sound, quality and length of each breath. Keep your breath flowing and your throat in the same position to channel the movement of energy into your body.
5. Continue breathing this way for 10 minutes, then slowly open your breath and return to normal breathing.

Right-nostril (*pingala*) breathing

This is a great way to give the body more energy.

1. Sit comfortably with your spine lengthened, your shoulders relaxed and your hands in your lap.
2. Take your right hand and block off your left nostril by putting gentle pressure on it with your right index finger. Keep your other right fingers straight and pointing toward the sky.
3. Gently inhale through your right nostril, taking a long, slow, deep breath.
4. Just as gently, exhale through your right nostril, slowly and completely.
5. Continue breathing this way for 10 minutes, relaxing your body and feeling the energy build smoothly and gracefully in your body, providing every cell with a new energy.

Left-nostril (*nadi*) breathing

This is very cooling for overheated pittas.

1. Sit comfortably with your spine lengthened, your shoulders relaxed and your hands in your lap.
2. Take your left hand and block off your right nostril by putting gentle pressure on it with your left index finger. Keep your other left fingers straight and pointing toward the sky.
3. Gently inhale through your left nostril, taking a long, slow, deep breath.
4. Just as gently, exhale through the left nostril, slowly and completely.
5. Continue breathing this way for 10 minutes, relaxing your body and feeling it cool down and become calm.

PART 3

Recipes for all seasons

A guide to the symbols

THE DOSHA SYMBOLS

Good things come in threes. Throughout the recipes in this book you'll find symbols that signify which dosha the recipe or content relates to. Look for your predominant dosha to find a recipe that's the most balancing for you. If you're a dual dosha type, for example, that means you can select recipes across both doshas, or you may be a bit of all three and parts of each dosha will resonate with you. Just keep an eye out for the signposts.

 Vata

 Pitta

 Kapha

Use these symbols as a guide to eating right for your shape. Once you've become more attuned to your dosha and its qualities, you'll be able to cultivate an intuitive understanding of what balances you and what will tip you further into the direction of imbalance. The blessing of a spiritual system of medicine such as Ayurveda is that it returns you to your innate wisdom, giving you the power to participate in a personal evolution and heal yourself through your daily choices.

THE TASTE SYMBOLS

Above each recipe you'll find a symbol with its accompanying tastes to help you to construct a recipe that's uniquely balanced for you.

 A   **Astringent**

 B   **Bitter**

 So   **Sour**

 P   **Pungent**

 Sa   **Salty**

 Sw   **Sweet**

THE FASTING SYMBOL

I've also included an icon to indicate whether the recipe is suitable for fasting days; just look out for this symbol.

Your shopping list

Make grocery shopping easy with this handy list. Two of the biggest hurdles to eating right for your shape are not having the right ingredients on hand and lack of time for preparation. Use the list appropriate for your dosha (see pages 28–33) to know which ingredients are going to work for you, then combine it with this full pantry list so that you know which foods you need to pick up each week. That means a lot less time wandering the aisles aimlessly, wondering if you need to buy broccoli or Brussels sprouts.

By having a list prepared, you can ensure you have everything you need to make the delicious recipes. Most of the ingredients can be found in your local supermarket or health food store, but you may need to go online or to your local spice market to find some of the spices. Buy as much organic as you can, and opt for grass-fed and -finished meats, free-range eggs and full-fat dairy.

VEGETABLES

Alfalfa sprouts (P) (K)
Artichokes (K)
Arugula (P) (K)
Asparagus (P) (K)
Bean sprouts (P) (K)
Beet greens (K)
Beets (V) (P)
Broccoli (P) (K)
Brown onions (P)
Brussels sprouts (K)
Butternut squash (V) (P)
Cabbage (P) (K)
Carrots (V) (P)
Cauliflower (P) (K)
Celery (K)
Chicory lettuce (P) (K)
Collard greens (P)
Cucumbers (P)
Eggplant (K)
Endive (K)

English spinach (V) (P) (K)
 (only in moderation for all doshas)
Fennel (V) (K)
French shallots (V) (P) (K)
Garlic (V) (K)
Green beans (V) (P) (K)
Green chilies (V) (K)
Green pepper (K)
Green onions (P)
Jerusalem artichokes (P) (K)
Kale (P) (K)
Kohlrabi (P) (K)
Leeks (V) (P) (K)
Mushrooms (P) (K)
Mustard greens (K)
Okra (P) (K)
Parsnips (K)
Peas (V) (K)
Potatoes (P) (K)

Radishes (K)
Red chilies (K)
Red-leaf lettuce (K)
Red onions (P) (K)
Red pepper (K)
Romaine lettuce (P) (K)
Rutabaga (V) (P)
Snow peas (V) (P)
Spaghetti squash (K)
Spring onions (scallions) (V) (P) (K)
Sprouts (all) (P) (K)
Squash (summer) (V) (P)
Sweet potato (V) (P) (K)
Swiss chard (P) (K)
Turnips (V) (P) (K)
Turnip greens (K)
Watercress (V) (K)
Winter squash (V) (P)
Zucchini (V) (P)

MEAT AND EGGS

Beef (V) (P)
Chicken (V) (P) (K)
Duck (V)
Eggs (V)
Egg whites (P) (K)
Ham and bacon (nitrate-free) (V)
Lamb (in moderation) (V) (P) (K)
Pheasant (P)
Pork (V)
Turkey (V) (P) (K)

SEAFOOD

Freshwater fish (V) (P) (K)
Salmon (wild-caught) (V) (P)
Tuna (V) (P) (K)
Sardines (V)
Sashimi (V) (P)
Scallops (V) (P) (K)
  (only in moderation for all doshas)
Sea vegetables (V)
Shrimp (V) (P)

DAIRY, DAIRY ALTERNATIVES AND DRINKS

Almond milk (V) (P)
Blue cheese (V)
Butter (unsalted) (P)
Coconut cream (V) (P)
Coconut milk (V) (P)
Cottage cheese (V)
Cream (V)
Full-fat cheddar cheese (V)
Full-fat cow's milk (V) (P)
Goat's cheese (V)
Goat's milk (V)
Kefir (V)

Kombucha (V)
Mozzarella (V)
Oat milk (V) (P)
Parmesan (V)
Rice milk (V) (K)
Romano cheese (V)
Sheep's cheese (V)
Soda water (P) (K)
Sour cream (V)
Soy milk (P)
Yogurt (plain, no additives) (V)

FATS, OILS AND CONDIMENTS

Almond oil (K)
  (in moderation)
Apple cider vinegar (V) (K)
Balsamic vinegar (V) (K)
Butter (V)
Cacao butter (V) (P)
Coconut butter (V) (P)
Coconut oil (extra virgin) (V) (P)
Flaxseed oil (V) (P)
Ghee (V) (P) (K)
  (in moderation)
Lard (V)
Mayonnaise, homemade (V) (P)
Miso (V)
Mustard (V) (K)
Mustard oil (K)

Olive oil (extra virgin, cold-pressed)
  (V) (K)
Pickles (V)
Safflower oil (V) (K)
Sauerkraut (V)
Sesame oil (V) (K)
Spirulina (K)
Stevia, liquid (K)
Stevia powder (K)
Sunflower oil (V)
Tahini (V)
Tallow (V)
Tomato paste (K)
Vegetable stock (sugar- and
  additive-free) (V) (P) (K)
Wheat-free tamari (V) (K)

SEEDS, NUTS AND NUT BUTTERS

Almond butter (V) (P)
Almonds (whole and slivered) (V) (P)
Brazil nuts (P)
Chia seeds (V) (P) (K)
 (in moderation)
Flaxseeds (linseed) (V) (P)

Hazelnuts (V)
Hemp seeds (V) (P)
Macadamias (P)
Pecans (K)
Pepitas (pumpkin seeds) (V) (P) (K)

Pine nuts (V)
Poppy seeds (V) (P)
Sesame seeds (V) (K)
Sunflower seeds (V) (P)
Walnuts (K)

GRAINS, FLOURS AND BAKING

Almond flour (V) (P)
Amaranth (P) (K)
Arrowroot (V) (P) (K)
Arrowroot powder (V) (P) (K)
Baking powder (gluten- and
 additive-free) (V) (P) (K)
Baking soda (V) (P) (K)
Barley (P) (K)
Basmati rice (V) (P) (K)
Brown rice and brown rice noodles (V) (K)
Brown rice crackers (V) (K)
Brown rice puffs (V) (P) (K)
Buckwheat (K)
Buckwheat groats, flour
 and pasta (K)
Coconut flakes and desiccated
 coconut (V) (P)
Coconut flour (V) (P)
Golden flaxmeal (V) (P)
Millet (K)
Oat bran (V) (P) (K)

Oat flour (V) (P)
Oatmeal (V) (K)
Oats (V) (P)
Polenta (K)
Popped corn (K)
Puffed rice (P) (K)
Quinoa (V) (P) (K)
Rice flour (V)
Rye (K)
Self-raising flour (gluten-free) (V) (P)
Sorghum (V) (P)
Spelt (V) (P)
Tapioca (V) (P)
Wheat (P)
Wheat, whole (V) (P)
White rice (only in moderation for
 all doshas) (V) (P) (K)
White rice flour (P)
Wild rice (V) (P) (K)

SWEETENERS

Cacao nibs (K)
Carob (K)
Coconut nectar (V) (P)
Coconut sugar (V) (P)
Honey (K)
Maple syrup (V) (P)
Molasses (V)
Pomegranate molasses (P)
Rapadura sugar (panela, jaggery) (V) (P)
Rice malt syrup (brown rice syrup) (V) (P)
Stevia, liquid (V) (P) (K)
Stevia powder (V) (P) (K)
Vanilla beans (V) (P)
Vanilla extract (alcohol-free) (K)
Xylitol (only in moderation for all
 doshas) (V) (P) (K)

FRUITS

- Apples (P) (K)
- Apples, cooked (V)
- Apricots (V) (K)
- Apricots, dried (V)
- Avocados (V) (P)
- Bananas (V) (P)
- Bitter melons (P) (K)
- Blackberries (fresh and frozen) (V) (P)
- Blueberries (fresh and frozen) (V) (P)
- Cherries (V) (K)
- Cherry tomatoes (K)
- Coconut (V)
- Cranberries (P) (K)
- Currants (P)
- Dates (P)
- Dates, soaked (V)
- Figs (V) (P)
- Goji berries (V) (P) (K)
- Grapefruit (V) (K)
- Grapes (V) (P)
- Green mango (P) (K)
- Guava (P)
- Kiwifruit (V)
- Lemon zest (P)
- Lemons (V) (K)
- Limes (V) (P) (K)
- Mandarins (V) (K)
- Mangoes (V)
- Melons (V) (P)
- Mulberries (V) (P)
- Nectarines (V)
- Olives (V)
- Oranges (V) (K)
- Papayas (V)
- Peaches (V) (P)
- Pears (K)
- Persimmons (V) (P)
- Pineapples (V) (P)
- Plums (V)
- Pomegranates (P) (K)
- Prunes (P) (K)
- Raisins (V) (P)
- Raspberries (fresh and frozen) (V) (P)
- Rhubarb (V) (P) (K)
- Strawberries (fresh and frozen) (V) (P) (K)
- Tamarind (V)
- Tomatoes (K)
- Watermelons (P) (K)

HERBS, SPICES AND TEAS

- Allspice (V) (K)
- Asafoetida (V) (K)
- Basil (V) (K)
- Bay leaves (V) (K)
- Black pepper (in moderation) (V) (P) (K)
- Black tea (K)
- Burdock (P) (K)
- Caraway seeds (V) (K)
- Cardamom (V) (P) (K)
- Cayenne pepper (V) (K)
- Celery seeds (K)
- Celtic sea salt (V)
- Chamomile (P) (K)
- Chickweed (K)
- Chili flakes (K)
- Chili powder (V) (K)
- Chinese cinnamon (in moderation) (P)
- Chives (V) (K)
- Cinnamon (V)
- Cloves (V)
- Cilantro (V) (P) (K)
- Coriander seeds (V) (P) (K)
- Cumin (in moderation) (V) (P) (K)
- Curry leaves (V) (K)
- Curry powder (V) (K)
- Dandelion (P) (K)
- Dill (in moderation) (V) (P) (K)
- Dulse flakes (V) (P) (K)
- Fennel seeds (V) (P) (K)
- Fenugreek (V) (K)
- Ginger, fresh (V) (P) (K)
- Ginger, ground (V) (K)
- Green tea (P) (K)
- Horseradish (K)
- Lavender (P) (K)
- Lemongrass (K)
- Marjoram (V) (K)
- Mint (P) (K)
- Mustard powder (V) (K)
- Mustard seeds (V) (K)
- Nigella seeds (charnushka) (V) (K)
- Nutmeg (V)
- Oregano (V) (K)
- Paprika (V) (K)
- Parsley (V) (K)
- Peppermint (P) (K)
- Rosemary (V) (K)
- Saffron (V) (P) (K)
- Sage (K)
- Spearmint (P) (K)
- Star anise (V) (K)
- Tarragon (V) (K)
- Thyme (V) (K)
- Turmeric (in moderation) (V) (P) (K)

LEGUMES (SOAKED/SPROUTED)

Adzuki beans (P) (K)
Black beans (P) (K)
Black-eyed peas (P) (K)
Broad (fava) beans (P) (K)
Butter beans (P) (K)
Cannellini beans (P) (K)

Chickpeas (garbanzo beans) (P) (K)
Kidney beans (P) (K)
Lentils (P) (K)
Mung beans (P) (K)
Navy beans (P) (K)

Pinto beans (P) (K)
Soya beans and edamame (P) (K)
Split peas (P) (K)
Tempeh (V) (P)
Tofu (V) (P)
Urad dal (P) (K)

FLOUR CHART

If you're wondering which gluten-free flour is best for your particular dosha or for balancing a dosha that's out of whack, this table will help.

Using neutral flours can keep the doshas balanced. Choose flours that bring your dominant dosha into balance, but remember moderation – you don't need to avoid a flour altogether, just reduce your use of it. For example, if you're a kapha, choosing flours that are neutral or reduce kapha, such as amaranth or buckwheat, will help. But if the flours that increase the dosha you're trying to bring into balance are mixed with other flours, you needn't avoid them completely.

Flour type	Vata	Pitta	Kapha
Almond	Reduces	Neutral	Increases
Amaranth	Neutral	Neutral	Reduces
Arrowroot	**Neutral**	**Neutral**	**Neutral**
Besan (chickpea)	Increases	Reduces	Reduces
Brown rice	Reduces	Increases	Neutral
Buckwheat	Increases	Increases	Reduces
Coconut	Reduces	Reduces	Increases
Corn	Increases	Increases	Reduces
Flaxseed	Reduces	Reduces	Increases
Millet	Increases	Increases	Reduces
Oat*	Neutral	Neutral	Neutral
Potato	Increases	Neutral	Decreases
Quinoa	Neutral	Neutral	Reduces
Sorghum	Reduces	Reduces	Increases
Sweet potato	Reduces	Reduces	Increases
Tapioca	Reduces	Reduces	Neutral
Taro	Reduces	Reduces	Increases
Teff	Increases	Increases	Reduces
White rice	Reduces	Reduces	Increases

* Gluten-free oats can still affect some people who are on a gluten-free diet.

Spring

Fling open the windows and rid yourself of winter layers with fresh and vibrant recipes embracing nature's bountiful springtime produce. Herald the day with a Minted Strawberry Slushie.

While breakfast is stirring and tummies are rumbling, whip up an Oven-baked Peach and Berry Pancake. Blossom, cleanse and renew with a light and appealing Liver-cleansing Green Dip or plant-based salad of colorful and crunchy Watercress, Fennel and Ruby Grapefruit.

Prepare yourself for the perfumed flavors of Oven-baked Saffron Chicken with Lime, and satisfy your tastebuds with Pistachio Truffles or heaven-scented Halva.

P 🔺B ▲P 🔺A ▲Sw

Omit the rice malt syrup

To balance vata, replace the dandelion with cacao powder

To balance kapha, replace the brazil nut milk with rice milk

BRAZIL NUT, DANDELION AND CARDAMOM LATTE

SERVES 1

In this exotic twist on a dandelion latte, the addition of aromatic and perfumed cardamom gives a wonderful Indian flavor. By adding brazil nuts you're injecting good fats and selenium into your body. Cardamom, a diaphoretic (inducing perspiration), is a powerful Ayurvedic mucus-demolisher suited to kapha types. It's a wonderful beauty-booster for all doshas, too, opening up your pores, encouraging a mild sweat and cleansing the lymphatic system.

BRAZIL NUT MILK
(makes 5 cups/44 fl oz/1.25 liters)
2 cups (10½ oz/300 g) **brazil nuts**
4 cups (35 fl oz/1 liter) **filtered water,**
    plus extra for soaking

LATTE
1 cup (9 fl oz/250 ml) **brazil nut milk**
1 teaspoon **rice malt syrup,**
    or stevia to taste
¼ cup (½ oz/15 g) **dandelion leaves**
    or 1 dandelion tea bag
large pinch of **ground cardamom**

To make the brazil nut milk, soak the brazil nuts in a large bowl of extra filtered water for 8 hours, then rinse and drain. Process the brazil nuts with the filtered water in a blender or food processor until smooth and creamy. Strain through a nut milk bag or fine sieve into a glass bottle and store in the fridge for 4–5 days. (The pulp can be used to make ice cream or baked goods the same day.)

To make the latte, combine the brazil nut milk and rice malt syrup in a small, heavy-based saucepan, add the dandelion leaves or tea bag and place over medium heat. Add the cardamom and stir for 2–3 minutes or until warmed through. Strain.

Transfer to a blender and blend until frothy, or use a hand-held frother. Pour into your favorite warmed mug, settle into an armchair and enjoy a little bit of the Taj Mahal in a cup.

CUP OF LIFE MORNING BROTH
SERVES 1

1 cup (9 fl oz/250 ml) vegetable stock (preferably homemade)
1 teaspoon Churna masala for your dosha (page 238)

Warm the stock in a saucepan over medium heat to a gentle simmer. Add the masala and stir to combine. Pour into a cup or bowl and enjoy mindfully.

KAPHA-BALANCING TEA
SERVES 3–4

4 cups (35 fl oz/1 liter) filtered water
1 tablespoon ground cinnamon
¼ teaspoon ground turmeric
1 teaspoon freshly grated ginger
6 drops liquid stevia or ⅛ teaspoon stevia powder

Warm the water in a saucepan over medium heat. Add the cinnamon and turmeric, bring to a boil, then continue boiling for 3 minutes, stirring constantly. Add the ginger and stevia, and boil for another 1 minute. Strain and serve hot.

L–R: Brazil nut, dandelion and cardamom latte (page 90); Minted strawberry slushie

To balance pitta, omit the cumin

DIGESTIVE LASSI
SERVES 2

Process all the ingredients in a blender until combined. Pour into two glasses and enjoy immediately.

2 cups (17 fl oz/500 ml) filtered water
½ cup (4½ oz/130 g) sheep's
    milk yogurt
1 inch (2.5 cm) piece of ginger,
    peeled and chopped
½ teaspoon cumin seeds or
    ground cumin
pinch of Celtic sea salt

To balance vata, omit the mint

MINTED STRAWBERRY SLUSHIE
SERVES 4

This is one of my favorite spring drinks and is a lovely livener for children. The strawberries inject sweetness, while the mint adds a subtle charm. In Ayurveda, mint helps disperse fluids and heat, which creates a cooling after-effect on the body. The aroma of mint can inspire and refresh the brain, and create a feeling of letting go. Kaphas can use this as a perky pick-me-up after a lazy afternoon at the beach.

Process the ice cubes and mint leaves in a food processor or blender to a slushy consistency. With the motor still running, add the strawberries and blend to break up. Pour in half the mineral or soda water and pulse to combine. Pour into a large jug, add the remaining water, stir and serve immediately.

2 large handfuls of ice cubes
2 mint sprigs, leaves picked
1 cup (5½ oz/150 g) strawberries, hulled
4 cups (35 fl oz/1 liter) sparkling mineral
    water or soda water

To balance kapha, replace the berries with chopped apple and the almond meal with buckwheat or brown rice flour

OVEN-BAKED PEACH AND BERRY PANCAKE
SERVES 3–4

In need of inspiration for breakfast? Then batter up! My fruity, easy-to-make peachy-keen baked pancake is bursting with flavor, thanks to the peach, berries and lemon zest, and can be whipped up in a matter of minutes. Added bonus: you don't have to wait near the stove to flip it; relax with a hot cup of tea and a good book while it bubbles in the oven, then enjoy it warm, topped with additional berries. These can also be made in four individual ramekins for a delicious warm "breakfast custard", and baked for 15–20 minutes.

1 tablespoon ghee, melted, for greasing
¾ cup (2¾ oz/80 g) almond meal
2 tablespoons (40 ml) rice malt syrup,
    plus extra to serve
½ teaspoon Celtic sea salt
4 eggs, lightly beaten
grated zest of 1 lemon
1 teaspoon alcohol-free vanilla extract
½ cup (4 fl oz/125 ml) almond
    or rice milk
1 large peach, sliced
1 cup (4½ oz/125 g) mixed berries,
    plus extra to serve

Preheat the oven to 400°F (200°C/gas mark 6) and grease a 10 inch (25 cm) ovenproof frying pan or baking dish with the ghee.

Put the almond meal, rice malt syrup, salt, eggs, lemon zest and vanilla in a medium bowl and whisk to combine. Gradually pour in the milk, whisking until smooth. Place the peach and berries in the prepared pan and pour the batter over the top.

Bake for 20–25 minutes or until puffed and golden. To serve, slice into wedges and top with extra rice malt syrup and berries.

V ▲ B ▲ P ▲ A ▲ Sw ▲ Sa ▲ So

To balance pitta, replace the nutmeg with cumin and use egg whites only

MICROHERB OMELETTE
SERVES 1

Microherbs can be purchased at your local market or in the fruit and vegetable section of your supermarket, but these little herbs are very easy to grow at home. Even if you live in an apartment you can create a windowsill vegetable garden using beets, cress, dill, amaranth, basil, linseed, mustard, pea, arugula, sunflower or barley grass. Microherbs are highly nutritious and can be added to smoothies and salads.

¾ oz (20 g) unsalted butter
¾ cup (2¼ oz/65 g) thinly
    sliced mushrooms
pinch of freshly grated nutmeg
Celtic sea salt and freshly cracked
    black pepper, to taste
handful of mixed microherbs
3 large eggs

Place a 8 inch (20 cm) frying pan over medium heat. Add half the butter and the mushrooms, and cook, stirring frequently, until the mushrooms are golden brown. Add the nutmeg, and season well with salt and pepper. Remove from the heat, transfer to a bowl and stir through the microherbs.

Break the eggs into a bowl and whisk until frothy.

Melt the remaining butter in the frying pan over medium heat, swirling to coat the base of the pan. Pour in the eggs, swirl them around to cover the base of the pan and cook for about 2 minutes or until just set. Spoon the mushroom mix onto one side of the omelette and fold over the other half. Slide the omelette onto a plate and serve immediately.

V ▲P ▲Sw ▲So

Omit the cashew nut cream and replace the rice malt syrup with 6 drops liquid stevia

To balance pitta, replace the cashew cream with coconut milk

To balance kapha, omit the cashew cream and replace the rice malt syrup with 6 drops liquid stevia

STEWED FRUITS WITH CASHEW CREAM
SERVES 2

To make the stewed fruit, place all the ingredients in a large, heavy-based saucepan over medium heat. Bring to a boil, stirring often, then reduce the heat to low and simmer, uncovered, for 10–15 minutes or until the fruit has formed a thick purée. Add more filtered water during cooking if necessary. Remove from the heat and set aside.

To make the cashew cream, rinse and drain the soaked cashews. Process all the ingredients in a food processor or blender until smooth and creamy. Add more filtered water if necessary to achieve a smooth consistency.

Divide the stewed fruits between two bowls and top each with a dollop of cashew cream. Sprinkle with sunflower seeds and serve.

2 tablespoons dry-roasted
   sunflower seeds, to serve

STEWED FRUIT
2 cups (10½ oz/300 g)
   strawberries, hulled
2 cups (9 oz/250 g) chopped rhubarb
2 tablespoons (40 ml) rice malt syrup
1 teaspoon ground cinnamon
1 cup (9 fl oz/250 ml) filtered water,
   plus extra as needed

CASHEW CREAM
1½ cups (8½ oz/235 g) raw cashews,
   soaked in filtered water for 2 hours
½ cup (4 fl oz/125 ml) filtered water,
   plus extra as needed
2 tablespoons (40 ml) rice malt syrup
juice of ½ lemon

To balance vata, use whole eggs and omit the cilantro leaves and coriander seeds

To balance pitta, omit the chili and replace the spinach with kale (optional); cooking onions in ghee is okay for pittas, as are small amounts of cooked spices such as turmeric and cumin

Note: All doshas can enjoy spinach in moderation

CUMIN SCRAMBLED EGGS AND GREENS
SERVES 2

The ideal kapha breakfast is a light and satisfying bowl of lightly scrambled eggs. By using just the egg whites in this recipe and bulking it up with a boost of healthy greens, you'll be adding a good punch of vitamins and minerals to boost kapha.

1 teaspoon ghee

1 teaspoon cumin seeds

½ teaspoon coriander seeds

½ teaspoon ground turmeric

2 small green chilies, seeded and finely chopped

½ red onion, finely chopped

⅓ red bell pepper, diced

4 egg whites

Celtic sea salt, to taste

2 cups (3¼ oz/90 g) baby spinach, wilted

small handful of cilantro leaves, to serve

Heat the ghee in a medium frying pan over medium heat. Add the cumin and coriander seeds and cook, stirring frequently, until they start to pop. Reduce the heat to low.

Add the turmeric and cook, stirring, for 1 minute. Add the chili, onion and pepper and cook for 2–3 minutes or until the onion is translucent.

In a bowl, lightly whisk the egg whites, season with salt, then pour into the pan. Stir with a fork until cooked to your liking. Serve on a bed of wilted spinach, with the cilantro on top.

V B A Sw Sa So

Note: Vatas should eat arugula only in moderation

To balance kapha, replace the carrot with zucchini noodles, sunflower seeds with sesame seeds, and rice malt syrup with 6 drops liquid stevia

To balance pitta, reduce the quantity of the dressing

CARROT, MANGO, ARUGULA AND SUNFLOWER SALAD WITH ORANGE DRESSING
SERVES 4

This dish is one of my favorite refreshing and tasty vata salads to take along to a party. I love to indulge in it on a warm spring day when there's a promise of even warmer days yet still a little bit of freshness in the air. I've included cooling, stimulating and blood-purifying carrots and oranges, and rice malt syrup to satisfy sweet cravings. These are countered beautifully by the crunchiness of the sunflower seeds and the bitterness of the arugula.

Toast the sunflower seeds in a dry, medium frying pan over medium–high heat. Transfer to a plate and set aside.

Return the frying pan to medium heat and add the orange zest, orange juice and rice malt syrup. Heat, stirring frequently, for 3–4 minutes, then pour into a bowl and set aside to cool.

Combine the carrot, arugula and mango in a large bowl. Pour over the cooled dressing, then fold through gently. Season with salt and pepper, top with the sunflower seeds and serve.

½ cup (2½ oz/75 g) **sunflower seeds**
finely grated zest of 3 **oranges**
1 cup (9 fl oz/250 ml) **orange juice**
2 tablespoons (40 ml) **rice malt syrup**
3 **carrots,** coarsely grated
2 cups (3¼ oz/90 g) **baby arugula,**
    torn or roughly chopped
2 **mangoes,** diced
Celtic sea salt and freshly cracked
    black pepper, to taste

V △ B ▲ P ▲ A ▲ Sw ▲ Sa ▲ So

To balance kapha, omit the carrot and avocado

To balance pitta, replace the brown rice with quinoa, cooked according to the package directions (10–12 minutes)

BROWN RICE NORI

MAKES 4

Vatas will enjoy this vegetarian version of a typical sushi roll, usually made with sweet white rice that can raise your blood sugar levels too quickly due to its sky-high glycemic index. By using wholesome brown rice and tempeh, you can create delicious rolls that will make your insides and outsides happy. The fiber in brown rice and fermented soy (tempeh and tamari) will ensure these rolls are easier for vatas' delicate bellies to digest. Bite down on raw cucumber and carrot to add crunchiness, and relish the creaminess of tahini and avocado, which add a dose of good fats to complete a balanced meal that's as fun to make as it is to eat.

¼ cup (2 fl oz/60 ml) wheat-free tamari, plus extra to serve

1 teaspoon lime juice

1 teaspoon ghee, melted

¼ cup (2¼ oz/65 g) tahini

3½ oz (100 g) tempeh

2 cups (13 oz/370 g) cooked brown rice

4 nori sheets

½ avocado, sliced

1 Lebanese (short) cucumber, sliced lengthwise into eighths

½ carrot, sliced lengthwise into thin sticks

2 spring onions (scallions), halved lengthwise

Combine the tamari, lime juice, ghee and 1 tablespoon (20 ml) of the tahini in a bowl. Add the tempeh and set aside to marinate for 10 minutes.

Remove the tempeh from the marinade. Heat a dry frying pan over medium heat and pan-fry the tempeh until golden on both sides. Cut into thin strips and set aside.

Combine the rice with the remaining tahini. Lay a nori sheet shiny side down on the counter. With wet hands, take a quarter of the rice and press it evenly over the nori sheet, leaving a 1¼ inch (3 cm) border along the top side. Lay a quarter of the tempeh, avocado, cucumber, carrot and spring onion on top. Moisten the top edge of the nori with water and roll up securely. Repeat with the remaining ingredients.

Cut each roll into four pieces and serve with extra tamari.

K ▲ P ▲ A ▲ Sw ▲ Sa ▲ So

Replace the ghee with apple cider vinegar

To balance pitta, replace the mustard with ground coriander and the tarragon
with cilantro leaves

ASPARAGUS WITH MUSTARD AND TARRAGON
SERVES 2

Preheat the oven to 400°F (200°C/gas mark 6).

Snap the woody ends off the asparagus. Place the asparagus in a roasting tin with the ghee and roast for 5 minutes or until the asparagus just begins to brown and is al dente.

Meanwhile, put the dressing ingredients in a glass jar, seal tightly and shake well to combine. Drizzle over the roasted asparagus and toss gently to coat. Top with the tarragon sprigs, season with pepper and serve.

2 bunches (12 oz/350 g) asparagus
1 tablespoon ghee, melted
a few tarragon sprigs, torn, to serve
freshly cracked black pepper, to serve

DRESSING
juice of ½ lime
1 teaspoon grated lime zest
1 tablespoon sugar-free mustard
1 tablespoon ghee, melted
6 drops liquid stevia (optional)
pinch of Celtic sea salt
2 teaspoons chopped tarragon

V P ▲ B ▲ P ▲ A ▲ Sw ▲ Sa ▲ So

LIVER-CLEANSING GREEN DIP
SERVES 3–4

Love your liver and it will love you back. Your largest internal organ has responsibility for a variety of important functions, including detoxification, so it's imperative to show your liver some loving. When the liver is clogged with toxins, it finds it hard to work, and that's when we can begin to feel sluggish and tired. My green dip is packed with as many as ten liver-cleansing ingredients for nurturing and nourishment this springtime.

1 large avocado

¼ cup (2 fl oz/60 ml) freshly squeezed lime juice

½ teaspoon Celtic sea salt

freshly cracked black pepper, to taste

chili flakes, to taste

1 tablespoon finely chopped cilantro leaves, plus extra whole leaves to serve

½ small red onion

2 garlic cloves

½ cup (2½ oz/75 g) brazil nuts, plus extra, finely chopped, to serve

2 cups (3¼ oz/90 g) baby spinach

1 tablespoon (20 ml) flaxseed oil

Flatbread (page 241), to serve

In a bowl, roughly mash the avocado flesh with a fork. Add 1 tablespoon (20 ml) of the lime juice, along with the salt, pepper, chili flakes and chopped cilantro.

Put the onion, garlic, brazil nuts, spinach, flaxseed oil and the remaining lime juice in a blender, and pulse to chop. You want the dip to be on the chunky side.

Add the mixture to the avocado and stir to combine. Cover and refrigerate until ready to use.

Top with chopped brazil nuts and cilantro leaves, and serve with the flatbread.

Omit the dressing and add 2 tablespoons (40 ml) lime juice, 1 tablespoon (20 ml) apple cider vinegar and 6 drops liquid stevia

Note: Vatas should reduce the quantity of the spinach; kaphas should halve the quantity of the dressing and replace the rice malt syrup with 6 drops liquid stevia

To balance pitta, omit the parsley and apple cider vinegar, and replace the pine nuts with pepitas (pumpkin seeds)

BABY SPINACH, PINE NUT AND POMEGRANATE SALAD
SERVES 6

To make the dressing, whisk all the ingredients in a bowl to combine.

Place all the salad ingredients in a bowl, then add the dressing, toss gently and serve.

6 cups (9½ oz/270 g) baby spinach, tough stems removed
1 red onion, diced
⅓ cup (1¾ oz/50 g) pine nuts, toasted in a dry frying pan
¼ cup (⅛ oz/5 g) flat-leaf (Italian) parsley
seeds of 1 pomegranate
Celtic sea salt, to taste

DRESSING
⅓ cup (2½ fl oz/80 ml) extra virgin olive oil
2 tablespoons (40 ml) rice malt syrup
1½ tablespoons (30 ml) filtered water
1 tablespoon (20 ml) lime juice
pinch of Celtic sea salt

K ▲ B ▲ P ▲ A ▲ Sw ▲ Sa ▲ So

Omit the olive oil

To balance vata, replace the watercress with steamed green beans

WATERCRESS, FENNEL AND RUBY GRAPEFRUIT SALAD

SERVES 4

2 pink grapefruit

⅛ teaspoon fennel seeds

2 tablespoons (40 ml) lemon juice

½ teaspoon finely grated lemon zest

1 tablespoon (20 ml) extra virgin olive oil

6 drops liquid stevia

½ teaspoon sugar-free brown mustard

pinch each of Himalayan salt and freshly
    cracked black pepper

1 small red onion, sliced

1 small bulb fennel, halved lengthwise
    and thinly sliced

3 cups (3¼ oz/90 g) watercress leaves

Reserving any juice, peel and slice the grapefruit, ensuring the pith is removed. Set aside ¼ cup (2 fl oz/60 ml) of the juice.

Heat a heavy-based frying pan over medium heat and toast the fennel seeds for a couple of minutes until they become fragrant. Grind them finely using a mortar and pestle.

Put the ground seeds, reserved grapefruit juice, lemon juice and zest, olive oil, stevia, mustard, salt and pepper in a glass jar. Seal tightly and shake well to combine.

Put the grapefruit slices, onion, fennel and watercress in a bowl, pour over the dressing and toss to combine.

V P ▲ B ▲ P ▲ A ▲ Sw ▲ Sa ▲ So

Note: Pittas should reduce the quantities of the spices and cashews, and omit the garlic if preferred

OATS UPMA
SERVES 2–3

Tempering is a traditional technique in Indian cooking whereby whole spices are pan-fried briefly in oil or ghee to liberate their essential oils and enhance and extract their full flavors. Tempering makes a dish more fragrant and flavorsome, bringing the essence of the spices to the fore and unlocking their healing capabilities.

To temper the spices, melt half the ghee in a heavy-based saucepan over medium heat. Add the mustard seeds and cook for 1 minute or until they begin to pop. Reduce the heat to low and add the remaining tempering spices, and the bay and curry leaves. Cook for about 30 seconds, then add the cashews (if using) and cook for another 30 seconds. Transfer to a bowl and set aside.

To prepare the upma, return the same pan to medium heat and melt the remaining ghee. Add the onion, ginger and chili, then cook for 4–5 minutes. Add the carrot, beans and peas, and cook, stirring frequently, for another 5 minutes. Stir through the turmeric.

Add the oats and water, increase the heat and bring to a boil. Cook for 3–4 minutes or as directed on the package, adding more water during cooking if necessary. Add salt to taste.

Serve topped with the tempered spice mix and cilantro.

1 tablespoon ghee

SPICES FOR TEMPERING
½ teaspoon mustard seeds
2 whole cloves
1 star anise
1 cardamom pod, crushed
½ cinnamon stick
1 bay leaf
10 curry leaves
4–5 cashews (optional)

UPMA
1 onion, thinly sliced
1 teaspoon freshly grated ginger
2 green chilies, seeded and chopped
1 carrot, diced
4½ oz (125 g) sliced green beans, cut on the diagonal
½ cup (2½ oz/ 75 g) peas (fresh or frozen)
½ teaspoon ground turmeric
1 cup (3¼ oz/ 95 g) gluten-free instant oats, toasted for 5 minutes in a dry frying pan and cooled
1½ cups (13 fl oz/ 375 ml) filtered water, plus extra as needed
Himalayan salt, to taste
1 tablespoon finely chopped cilantro leaves, to serve

V P K ▲ B ▲ P ▲ A ▲ A ▲ Sw ▲ Sa ▲ So

Note: Pittas should halve the quantities of the spices; kaphas should use ghee and omit the nutmeg

ANTI-INFLAMMATORY SPRING PEA SOUP
SERVES 4-6

Heat the coconut oil in a large saucepan over low heat. Add the onion and cook for 5 minutes or until softened.

Add the stock, increase the heat to medium and bring to a boil. Add the peas and cook for 3–5 minutes or until tender (frozen peas need half that cooking time). Add the lemon juice, herbs, spices, salt and pepper, and stir to combine.

Remove from the heat, allow to cool slightly, then purée to your preferred consistency in a blender or food processor.

Serve sprinkled with sunflower seeds and topped with extra mint and parsley leaves.

2 tablespoons extra virgin coconut oil or ghee
1 onion, chopped
4 cups (35 fl oz/1 liter) vegetable stock (preferably homemade)
5 cups (1 lb 9 oz/700 g) peas (fresh or frozen)
1 tablespoon (20 ml) lemon juice
handful of mint, chopped, plus extra leaves to serve
handful of flat-leaf (Italian) parsley, chopped, plus extra leaves to serve
½ teaspoon ground cumin
pinch of freshly grated nutmeg
2 teaspoons Celtic sea salt
½ teaspoon freshly cracked black pepper
sunflower seeds, toasted in a dry frying pan, to serve

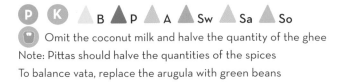

P K ▲ B ▲ P ▲ A ▲ Sw ▲ Sa ▲ So

Omit the coconut milk and halve the quantity of the ghee

Note: Pittas should halve the quantities of the spices

To balance vata, replace the arugula with green beans

CREAM OF ARUGULA SOUP
SERVES 3

A creamy, detoxifying soup for improved digestion. Rich in phytochemicals, antioxidants, fiber and essential minerals, arugula helps cleanse toxins from the body. Its sharp, peppery and bitter flavor is a sign that it's light and easy to digest, making this soup the perfect dinner for spring, when the body needs lighter food. Thanks to the mix of spices, this delicious and cleansing soup combines flavors and ingredients suitable for pittas and kaphas.

1 tablespoon ghee

2 whole cloves

½ cinnamon stick

1 bay leaf

6 curry leaves (optional)

1 onion, finely chopped

3 garlic cloves, finely chopped

¼ teaspoon finely chopped ginger

1 green chili, seeded and finely chopped

4 cups (5 oz/140 g) arugula leaves

4 cups (35 fl oz/1 liter) vegetable stock (preferably homemade)

¼ cup (2 fl oz/60 ml) additive-free coconut milk

Celtic sea salt and freshly cracked black pepper, to taste

Heat the ghee in a large saucepan over medium heat. Add the cloves, cinnamon stick, bay leaf and curry leaves (if using), and fry for 30 seconds. Add the onion, garlic, ginger and chili, and cook for 3–4 minutes or until the onion is translucent. Add the arugula leaves and cook, stirring frequently, for 2–3 minutes or until wilted. Add the stock, bring to a simmer and cook for 5–10 minutes.

Remove from the heat, allow to cool slightly, then remove and discard the cloves, cinnamon stick, bay leaf and curry leaves. Process the remaining mixture in a blender or food processor until smooth.

Return to the pan, add the coconut milk and reheat gently. Season with salt and pepper, and serve.

Note: Pittas should halve the quantities of the spices

OVEN-BAKED SAFFRON CHICKEN WITH LIME
SERVES 6

Preheat the oven to 475°F (240°C/gas mark 9).

Rinse the chicken inside and out and pat dry with paper towel.

Pound the saffron, salt, pepper, garlic and ginger to a paste using a mortar and pestle.

Place the chicken in a roasting tin and rub over the olive oil (if using) and lime juice. Rub the spice paste over the chicken, placing some in the cavity as well. Pour the water into the roasting tin. Cover the tin with foil and place in the oven, lowering the heat to 400°F (200°C/gas mark 6).

Roast the chicken for 60–75 minutes or until the juices run clear when the flesh is pierced with a skewer. Baste regularly, adding more water if necessary.

Allow to rest for 10–15 minutes before carving. Serve with the green bean subji and quinoa pilau.

3 lb 5 oz (1.5 kg) chicken
1 teaspoon saffron threads
1 teaspoon Himalayan salt
¼ teaspoon freshly cracked black pepper
4 garlic cloves, crushed
1 inch (2.5 cm) piece of ginger, peeled and finely chopped
1 tablespoon (20 ml) extra virgin olive oil (optional)
⅓ cup (2½ fl oz/80 ml) lime juice
½ cup (4 fl oz/125 ml) filtered water, plus extra as needed
Green bean subji (page 136) and Quinoa pilau (page 222), to serve

V K ▲B ▲P ▲A ▲Sw ▲Sa ▲So

INDIAN INFUSED CHICKEN
SERVES 4

3 lb 5 oz (1.5 kg) chicken
Baby spinach, pine nut and pomegranate
    salad (page 107), to serve

INDIAN INFUSED MARINADE
2 garlic cloves, crushed
½ onion, finely chopped
2 tablespoons (40 ml) lemon juice
2 tablespoons (40 ml) sesame oil
2 tablespoons brown rice flour
2 tablespoons finely chopped
    cilantro leaves
1 tablespoon ground cumin
2 teaspoons freshly grated ginger
2 teaspoons Himalayan salt
1 teaspoon garam masala
1 teaspoon sweet paprika
½ teaspoon chili powder
1–2 tablespoons (20–40 ml) warm
    filtered water

To make the marinade, combine all the ingredients with sufficient warm water to make a paste of spreading consistency.

Rub the marinade over the chicken, ensuring it is completely covered. Place in a roasting tin, cover with foil and marinate in the fridge for at least 1 hour but preferably overnight.

Preheat the oven to 350°F (180°C/gas mark 4).

Remove the foil and roast the chicken for 75–90 minutes or until the juices run clear when the flesh is pierced with a skewer. If the chicken starts to brown too much during cooking, cover with fresh foil. Rest for 10–15 minutes before serving.

Serve warm with baby spinach, pine nut and pomegranate salad. The chicken will be very moist and tender, and won't be spicy-hot.

Indian infused chicken with baby spinach, pine nut and pomegranate salad (page 107)

V ▲ B ▲ P ▲ A ▲ Sw ▲ Sa ▲ So ⬛

To balance pitta, replace the lamb with chicken and halve the quantities of the spices

To balance kapha, replace the lamb with chicken

SPICY LAMB KOFTAS
SERVES 4 (MAKES 8 KOFTAS)

Preheat a chargrill pan or barbecue hotplate to medium.

To make the koftas, mix all the ingredients in a bowl until well combined. Divide the mixture into eight portions and form each into a short sausage shape. Thread each onto a bamboo skewer and refrigerate for 15 minutes.

Place the skewers on the prepared pan or hotplate and cook for 10 minutes, turning halfway through.

Serve with a garden salad and the coconut relish.

8 bamboo skewers, soaked in water for 30 minutes
garden salad and Coconut relish (page 237), to serve

KOFTAS
1 lb 2 oz (500 g) ground lamb
1 small brown onion, chopped
2 garlic cloves, crushed
1 inch (2.5 cm) piece of ginger, peeled and grated
1 tablespoon chopped mint
1 tablespoon chopped flat-leaf (Italian) parsley
1 teaspoon mild paprika
1 teaspoon ground cumin
1 teaspoon ground turmeric
1 teaspoon ground coriander
Celtic sea salt, to taste

To balance pitta, replace the lamb or beef with chicken, replace the pilau with Vegetable thoran (page 182), reduce the quantities of the spices and omit the chili and black pepper

To balance kapha, replace the lamb or beef with chicken, replace the pilau with Tamatar salat (page 139) and halve the quantity of the sheep's milk yogurt

KEEMA MATAR (MINCE WITH PEAS)
SERVES 4

2 tablespoons ghee
1 large onion, thinly sliced
4 garlic cloves, crushed
1½ teaspoons freshly grated ginger
1 teaspoon freshly grated turmeric or ground turmeric
½ teaspoon chili powder
2 teaspoons ground cumin
½ teaspoon Himalayan salt
1 lb 2 oz (500 g) ground lamb or beef
¾ cup (7 oz/200 g) sheep's milk yogurt
1½ cups (6¾ oz/195 g) frozen baby peas
2 teaspoons garam masala (optional)
freshly cracked black pepper, to taste
filtered water (optional), for moistening
Spiced basmati pilau (page 245), to serve
large handful of cilantro leaves, chopped
almonds, roughly chopped, to serve

Heat the ghee in a wok or heavy-based frying pan over medium heat. Add the onion and cook for 3–4 minutes or until soft. Add the garlic and ginger, and cook for 2 minutes, taking care not to burn the garlic. Add the turmeric, chili, cumin and salt, and stir for a few seconds.

Add the meat and cook, stirring frequently, until it breaks up and browns. Stir through the yogurt and peas, then reduce the heat to low and cook, covered, for 15 minutes. Stir through the garam masala (if using) and pepper to taste. If you prefer a moist dish, add some filtered water.

Serve with the pilau, with cilantro and almonds scattered on top.

L–R: Keema matar;
Spiced basmati pilau
(page 245)

L–R: Pistachio truffles; Halva

Note: Kaphas should eat this only in small quantities

HALVA
SERVES 4–6

This healing sweet will comfort and energize. It's especially beneficial for vata; the warming nature of sesame seeds helps retain body heat, moisturise the hair and skin, promote better digestion and lubricate the intestines. The addition of rice malt syrup makes it a low-fructose delicacy to enjoy mindfully.

Line a 4½ inch (12 cm) square cake pan or other container with parchment paper.

Mix the tahini, sesame seeds, rice malt syrup, vanilla and cardamom together in a bowl, then press the mixture into the prepared cake pan and cut into squares or lozenge shapes. Place an almond on top of each piece.

Serve sprinkled with salt (if using).

⅓ cup (3¼ oz/90 g) raw tahini
⅓ cup (1¾ oz/50 g) sesame seeds
2 tablespoons (40 ml) rice malt syrup
1 teaspoon alcohol-free vanilla extract or ½ teaspoon vanilla powder
1 teaspoon ground cardamom
almonds, to serve
pinch of Himalayan salt (optional), to serve

PISTACHIO TRUFFLES
MAKES 24

Pulse all the ingredients except the shredded coconut in a food processor until smooth. Use your hands to roll tablespoons of the mixture into balls. Roll in the shredded coconut and refrigerate until ready to serve.

1 cup (9 fl oz/250 ml) additive-free coconut milk
4½ oz (125 g) cashew butter
½ cup (2¼ oz/65 g) coconut flour
1 cup (5 oz/140 g) pistachio kernels
½ cup (2½ oz/75 g) sesame seeds
½ cup (2½ oz/75 g) sunflower seeds
2½ tablespoons rice malt syrup
1 teaspoon vanilla powder
1 teaspoon ground cardamom
pinch of Himalayan salt
shredded coconut, for rolling

Summer

Summer brings with it some delicious and inspired recipes that are best consumed al fresco. Relax and sip on a Blueberry and Lavender Smoothie, or chill your pitta with an Iced Rose Tea.

Banana, Raspberry and Flax Breakfast Whip and Summer Breakfast Parfait are both a quick and easy start to the day, and will fill you up with antioxidant-rich goodness. Snack on Spiced Pecans or Cassava Chips, and dine on aromatic Tea-poached Chicken with Green Beans or Baked Fish with Flaxseed Crust.

Lay out your afternoon-tea summer entertaining table and delight guests with Coconut Bark with Rosewater, Pistachios and Raspberries or light and squidgy Aloe Vera Jelly.

L–R: Chill your pitta rose petal tea; Saffron lemonade

P △ B △ A △ Sw △ So ◉

CHILL YOUR PITTA ROSE PETAL TEA
SERVES 4

Prepare the rosewater the day before you want to serve the tea.

In a heavy-based saucepan, bring the water to a boil. Add the rose petals and lime juice, then turn off the heat, cover and allow to infuse overnight.

The next day, strain the rosewater into a large jug. Discard the petals.

To make the tea, place the tea bags in a teapot and bring the water to the boil. Pour the water over the tea, then add the rice malt syrup.

Allow the tea to cool then add the 2 teaspoons rosewater. Stir to combine.

Serve chilled over ice.

ROSEWATER
3 cups (26 fl oz/750 ml) filtered water
3 large unsprayed roses, petals only, white bases removed
½ teaspoon lime juice

TEA
2 decaf tea bags
2 cups (17 fl oz/500 ml) filtered water
1 tablespoon (20 ml) rice malt syrup or sweetener of your choice
2 teaspoons rosewater (see above)
ice cubes, to serve

V K △ B △ A △ Sw △ So ◉

To balance pitta, replace the lemon with lime

SAFFRON LEMONADE
SERVES 1

Heat the saffron in a bowl over a saucepan of boiling water. Remove from the heat and pound using a mortar and pestle to break up. Add 2 tablespoons (40 ml) warm water and set aside for 15–20 minutes.

Transfer to a large glass or a bottle, then add the lemon juice and mineral water. Add stevia and serve immediately over ice.

pinch of saffron threads
juice of 1 lemon
1 cup (9 fl oz/250 ml) sparkling mineral water or soda water
6 drops liquid stevia or to taste
ice cubes, to serve

V ▲ B ▲ A ▲ Sw

Omit the sesame seeds

To balance pitta, omit the sesame seeds

To balance kapha, replace the almond milk with rice milk

BLUEBERRY AND LAVENDER SMOOTHIE

SERVES 1

Here comes summer. This delicious smoothie is like a big bowl of fresh air filling your lungs and mind with goodness. The indigo-hued blueberries and lavender blossoms make it light and refreshing, the perfect breakfast for a warm summery day. In Ayurvedic medicine, blueberries help relieve an overheated mind and calm random thoughts. They also help to move energy downward and inward, which is thought to tame pitta and encourage a more passive demeanour. The sesame seeds and almond milk provide a creaminess that will envelop your senses and leave you feeling blissfully satisfied.

1 cup (9 fl oz/250 ml) almond milk
½ cup (2¾ oz/80 g) blueberries
2 tablespoons toasted sesame seeds
pinch of food-grade dried lavender

Process all the ingredients in a blender until smooth. Serve immediately.

SUMMER SMOOTHIE
SERVES 2

This refreshing, thick and satisfying smoothie is the perfect breakfast or afternoon pick-me-up on a hot summer's day. The sweetness of the banana and coconut are beautifully matched by the tanginess of the lime. It's the ideal drink to pacify vata and cool pitta.

Process all the ingredients in a blender on low speed until smooth. Serve immediately.

2 cups (17 fl oz/500 ml) coconut water
2 frozen peeled bananas
2 tablespoons (40 ml) lime juice
1 tablespoon grated lime zest
¼ teaspoon ground cardamom

BANANA, RASPBERRY AND FLAX BREAKFAST WHIP
SERVES 2

Process all the ingredients in a blender on high speed for 1 minute or until smooth. Serve immediately.

2 cups (17 fl oz/500 ml) almond milk
2 bananas, peeled
juice of ½ lime
1 cup (4½ oz/125 g) raspberries
2 teaspoons flaxseeds (linseed)
½ teaspoon ground cardamom
3 ice cubes

V P ▲A ▲Sw

To balance kapha, replace the coconut milk with sheep's milk yogurt, and omit the coconut flakes and almond butter

SUMMER BREAKFAST PARFAIT
SERVES 3

You know those lazy summer mornings when you wake up hungry but don't want to overload your body with a heavy breakfast? My solution for a cool, calm start to the day is a replenishing layered parfait to beat the summer heat. I've included luscious berries, known for their soothing effect on vatas' and pittas' overheated minds, providing grounding energy to quieten thoughts down.

14 fl oz (2 × 400 ml) cans additive-free coconut milk, chilled overnight in the fridge

1 teaspoon alcohol-free vanilla extract

1⅔ cups (9 oz/250 g) strawberries, hulled and sliced

½ cup (2½ oz/75 g) sunflower seeds

1⅔ cups (9 oz/255 g) blueberries

⅓ cup (¾ oz/20 g) coconut flakes, toasted (optional)

3¼ oz (90 g) almond butter, melted, for drizzling

Skim the cream from the top of the coconut milk and place in a small mixing bowl. (Reserve the remaining liquid in the bottom of the cans for use in smoothies.) Add the vanilla and whip the cream using hand-held beaters on high until it is thick, with the consistency of whipped cream.

Place 2 tablespoons of the coconut cream in each of three tall glasses. Using one-third of the strawberries, add a layer to each glass. Using one-quarter of the sunflower seeds, add a layer to each glass, then using one-third of the blueberries, add a layer to each glass, followed by another layer of sunflower seeds using another one-quarter. Repeat these layers of cream, strawberries, seeds, blueberries and seeds. Add a last layer of the remaining whipped cream, then garnish with the remaining berries and with the coconut flakes (if using). Top with the melted almond butter, sprinkle over the remaining sunflower seeds and serve immediately.

V ▲B ▲P ▲A ▲Sw ▲Sa

To balance pitta, use egg white only

To balance kapha, use egg white only, and replace the coconut flour with tapioca flour and blueberries with strawberries; sprinkle with stevia instead of using the cardamom coconut cream

PISTACHIO AND BLUEBERRY PANCAKES
SERVES 3–4

Vatas will discover the sweet deliciousness of these light and fantastically healthy pancakes. Coconut flour is packed with fiber for a healthy digestive fire (*agni*) and cleansed liver. Ayurveda holds that an agitated liver should be dampened and soothed with good fats, and pampered with sweet, delightful flavors such as coconut. The sweetness and freshness of blueberries complement the earthy crunchiness of the pistachios enormously. Enjoy with the coconut cream given here or my Lemony Coconut Mousse (page 232).

To make the cardamom coconut cream, skim the cream from the top of the coconut milk and place in a small mixing bowl. (Reserve the remaining liquid in the bottom of the can for use in smoothies.) Add the remaining ingredients and whip the cream using hand-held beaters on high until it is thick, with the consistency of whipped cream.

Break the eggs into a medium bowl and whisk until frothy. Stir in the milk and vanilla. Sift the flour, baking soda and salt into the egg mixture. Add the stevia and stir until combined. Fold in the blueberries and pistachios.

Heat a large frying pan over medium heat and add enough coconut oil to coat the base. Once the pan is hot, add ¼ cup (2 fl oz/60 ml) dollops of the mixture and cook until bubbles form on the surface, then flip and cook the other side. Repeat with the remaining batter.

Serve topped with the strawberries, cardamom coconut cream and a drizzle of rice malt syrup.

4 eggs
1½ cups (13 fl oz/375 ml) almond milk
2 teaspoons alcohol-free vanilla extract
½ cup (2¼ oz/65 g) coconut flour
1 teaspoon baking soda
¼ teaspoon Celtic sea salt
stevia, to taste
1 cup (5½ oz/155 g) blueberries
⅔ cup (3¼ oz/90 g) pistachio kernels, finely chopped
extra virgin coconut oil, for shallow-frying
strawberries, cut in half, to serve
rice malt syrup, to serve

CARDAMOM COCONUT CREAM
14 fl oz (400 ml) can additive-free coconut milk, chilled overnight in the fridge
½ teaspoon ground cardamom
½ teaspoon alcohol-free vanilla extract
½ teaspoon ground cinnamon
stevia, to taste

To balance pitta, omit the apple cider vinegar, replace the buckwheat flour with tapioca flour
and the rice milk with almond milk, and reduce the quantity of the salt
To balance vata, replace the buckwheat flour with tapioca flour and the rice milk with almond milk

BANANA AND BUCKWHEAT HOTCAKES
MAKES 8

Buckwheat hotcakes are suitably filling, and a flipping good source of fiber, magnesium
and amino acids, which makes them an ideal breakfast for speeding up a kapha's slow-
paced morning. Your appetite will be satisfied and your sweet tooth appeased, ready
for a flat-out day. These will puff up into billowy, pillowy fluffy pancakes.

1 cup (4½ oz/130 g) buckwheat flour
½ teaspoon Celtic sea salt
½ teaspoon baking powder
¼ teaspoon baking soda
1 cup (9 fl oz/250 ml) rice milk
1 tablespoon (20 ml) apple cider vinegar
6 drops liquid stevia or 1 tablespoon
    (20 ml) rice malt syrup
1 egg white
1 large banana, peeled and mashed,
    plus extra sliced banana to serve
1 tablespoon ghee
rice malt syrup, to serve
¼ cup (1½ oz/40 g) sunflower seeds,
    toasted in a dry frying pan, to serve

Sift the flour, salt, baking powder and baking soda into a
medium bowl. In another bowl, combine the milk, apple cider
vinegar, stevia, egg white and banana, and stir well. Add the wet
ingredients to the dry ingredients and stir well to combine.

Heat a large frying pan over medium heat. Add the ghee and
swirl to coat the base of the pan.

Add ¼ cup (2 fl oz/60 ml) dollops of the mixture to the pan
and cook until bubbles form on the surface, then flip and cook
the other side. Repeat with the remaining batter.

Top with the extra banana, drizzle over the rice malt syrup
and sprinkle with the sunflower seeds.

P ▲ A ▲ Sw

Omit the coconut flakes

To balance vata, add a pinch of Celtic sea salt to the oatmeal

PITTA-PACIFYING OATMEAL WITH SUMMER FRUITS

SERVES 2

In a medium saucepan over high heat, combine the oats with the water and bring to a boil, stirring constantly. Reduce the heat to low and continue to cook until the oats reach a soft, even, creamy consistency and have absorbed all the water. Add the vanilla and stevia.

Spoon into bowls and top with the berries and toasted coconut flakes.

1 cup (3¼ oz/95 g) gluten-free rolled oats

3 cups (26 fl oz/750 ml) filtered water

½ teaspoon alcohol-free vanilla extract

6 drops liquid stevia or 1 tablespoon (20 ml) rice malt syrup

1 cup (4½ oz/125 g) mixed berries (blackberries, blueberries, strawberries, raspberries)

¼ cup (½ oz/15 g) coconut flakes, toasted in a dry frying pan

B ▲P ▲A ▲Sw ▲Sa ▲So

Note: Pittas should reduce the quantities of the spices

Omit the coconut and use only 1 teaspoon ghee

To balance kapha, omit the coconut

GREEN BEAN SUBJI

SERVES 4-6

Whoever said vegetables are boring and time-consuming needs a rap across the pork knuckles. This delicious side dish will sit front and center on the dining table and can be made in minutes. It's bursting with flavor, thanks to the addition of traditional and exotic Indian spices. The coconut gives it a subtly sweet taste that will turn this simple green bean dish into the hero. Green beans are regarded in Ayurveda as one of the only beans not to aggravate sensitive vata.

2 tablespoons ghee or extra virgin
    olive oil
½ teaspoon cumin seeds
½ teaspoon black mustard seeds
¼ teaspoon ground turmeric
½ teaspoon Churna masala for your
    dosha (page 238)
½ onion, chopped
1 inch (2.5 cm) piece of ginger, peeled
    and finely chopped
2 garlic cloves, chopped
1 tablespoon shredded coconut
2 tablespoons chopped cilantro leaves
1 lb 2 oz (500 g) green beans, sliced
filtered water, as needed (optional)
½ teaspoon Celtic sea salt

Heat the ghee in a medium frying pan over medium heat. Add the cumin seeds and mustard seeds, and cook until the mustard seeds have popped. Add the turmeric, churna masala and onion, and cook for 3–4 minutes or until the onion is translucent.

Stir through the ginger, garlic, coconut and cilantro, then add the beans. Reduce the heat to low, then cover and cook until the beans are soft, adding a little filtered water if it gets too dry.

Season with salt and serve.

L–R: Spiced pecans; Tamatar salat

K ▲ P ▲ A ▲ Sw ▲ Sa

SPICED PECANS
MAKES 2 CUPS

Preheat the oven to 315°F (160°C/gas mark 2.5) and line a baking sheet with parchment paper.

Combine the ghee, rice malt syrup, spices and salt in a medium bowl and stir well. Add the pecans and toss to coat in the spice mixture.

Spread out the pecans on the prepared baking sheet and bake for 15–20 minutes or until golden, stirring a few times during cooking.

Remove from the oven and allow to cool, then store in an airtight container.

1 tablespoon ghee, melted
2 tablespoons (40 ml) rice malt syrup
½ teaspoon ground cinnamon
½ teaspoon vanilla powder
⅛ teaspoon cayenne pepper
1 teaspoon Celtic sea salt
2 cups (7 oz/200 g) pecans

K ▲ B ▲ P ▲ A ▲ Sw ▲ Sa ▲ So

 Replace the sesame oil with apple cider vinegar and use stevia rather than rice malt syrup

Note: Kaphas should use sesame oil only in small quantities; all doshas should eat tomato only in moderation

TAMATAR SALAT
SERVES 2–3

Combine the lemon juice, salt, pepper, rice malt syrup and sesame oil in a bowl. Add the tomato and reserved juice, onion and herbs, then toss gently to combine.

Serve at room temperature.

¼ cup (2 fl oz/60 ml) freshly squeezed lemon or lime juice
2 teaspoons Himalayan salt
freshly cracked black pepper, to taste
1 teaspoon rice malt syrup or 6 drops liquid stevia
2 teaspoons sesame oil
4 ripe tomatoes, diced, juices reserved
½ onion, finely chopped
2 tablespoons finely chopped cilantro leaves
2 tablespoons roughly chopped mint

Note: All doshas should eat tomato only in moderation

EGGPLANT BHARTA
SERVES 2

This kapha-balancing shaggy mash that can be eaten cold as a dip is perfect as a side dish or entrée. I encourage you to make a few serves ahead of time and keep it in the fridge to be enjoyed as a snack with batons of raw carrot, celery and cucumber.

1 large eggplant
extra virgin olive oil, for brushing
1 tablespoon ghee
1 teaspoon cumin seeds
1 small onion, finely chopped
2.5 cm (1 inch) piece of ginger, peeled
    and grated
2 garlic cloves, crushed
½ small green chili, seeded and
    finely chopped
1 tomato, finely chopped (to yield ½ cup)
½ teaspoon ground turmeric
½ teaspoon ground coriander
1 teaspoon ground cumin
½ teaspoon garam masala
Celtic sea salt, to taste
2 tablespoons finely chopped cilantro
    leaves, to serve (optional)
Indian dosas (page 240), to serve

Cut three or four slits in the eggplant, then brush the eggplant with a little olive oil. Heat a medium frying pan over medium heat, then fry the eggplant for 10 minutes, turning frequently, until it is soft and charred. Remove from the heat. When cool enough to handle, remove and discard the skin. Mash the flesh and set aside.

Heat the ghee in a clean frying pan over medium heat and add the cumin seeds. Cook for 1 minute, then add the onion and cook for another minute. Add the ginger, garlic and chili, then cook, stirring frequently, for 1 minute. Add the tomato and ground turmeric, coriander and cumin, then continue to cook, stirring frequently, for 3 minutes. Add the mashed eggplant, garam masala and salt. Stir to combine and cook for another 2 minutes.

Top with the cilantro leaves (if using) and serve with Indian dosas.

L–R: Indian dosas (page 240); Eggplant bharta

Note: Kaphas should eat goat's milk yogurt only in moderation

DAIKON AND CHICORY SALAD
SERVES 4

Raw daikon is rich in digestive enzymes, which makes it the perfect addition to any meal, especially for those with a weak digestive system. Another interesting vegetable, chicory will gently cleanse your body and improve your gut function. Daikon and chicory work wonderfully together to flush waste and toxins out of the body, support the detoxification process and enhance digestive function by stimulating bile production in the liver, which in turn helps in the digestion of fats. The yogurt and tahini dressing, with its Indian and Middle Eastern spices, enriches the dish and adds a creamy texture.

Combine all the dressing ingredients in a bowl and whisk well. Refrigerate until ready to use.

Arrange the vegetables on serving plates and pour over the dressing. Season with pepper, then top with the hazelnuts, cilantro and mint, and serve.

4 cups (12¾ oz/360 g) grated or
    spiralised daikon
2 chicory/Belgian endives, chopped
1 zucchini, grated or spiralized
freshly cracked black pepper, to taste
chopped hazelnuts, to serve
chopped cilantro leaves,
    to serve
chopped mint, to serve

DRESSING
1 cup (9¼ oz/260 g) goat's milk yogurt
½ cup (4¾ oz/135 g) tahini
grated zest and juice of 1 orange
2 tablespoons (40 ml) apple cider vinegar
1 tablespoon (20 ml) rice malt syrup
    or 6 drops liquid stevia
1 teaspoon ground cumin
1 teaspoon ground coriander
½ teaspoon freshly grated ginger
½ teaspoon ground turmeric
½ teaspoon ground cinnamon
pinch of cayenne pepper

CASSAVA CHIPS
SERVES 3–4

2 cassava, peeled
extra virgin coconut oil, for deep-frying
Himalayan salt, to taste

Wash the cassava under running water and pat dry. Cut into very thin slices using a mandolin or a very sharp knife.

Meanwhile, heat the coconut oil over medium–high heat in a deep, heavy-based saucepan until it reaches a temperature of 350°F (180°C/gas mark 4) or a cassava slice cooks in 1 minute.

Carefully drop the cassava slices into the pan and cook for 1 minute or until golden. You will need to do this in batches. Remove them carefully using a slotted spoon and lay on paper towel to drain off any excess oil.

Sprinkle with salt and serve immediately.

To balance vata, replace the vegetables with 4 cups (1 lb 2 oz/500 g) sliced green beans and omit the lime zest
To balance pitta, omit the spinach

DIGESTION SOUP
SERVES 4

This soup made with summer vegetables is a kapha secret weapon for detoxifying and alkalizing your body, giving your gut a rest to enhance digestion, and still providing all the nutrients your body needs to thrive. Ginger, lime and cilantro will assist your digestion while almond milk will add a delicious creaminess that will cleanse and renew your body.

Heat the olive oil in a large saucepan over medium heat. Add the ginger and churna masala, and cook for 1 minute or until fragrant. Add the vegetables and milk, then bring to a boil. Reduce the heat to low and simmer for 15 minutes.

Remove from the heat and allow to cool slightly, then transfer to a blender or food processor, add the lime juice and purée until smooth.

Season with salt and pepper, top with cilantro and serve.

1 teaspoon extra virgin olive oil or ghee
1 inch (2.5 cm) piece of ginger, peeled and finely chopped
2 teaspoons Churna masala for your dosha (page 238)
1 small head of broccoli, chopped
½ cauliflower, chopped
4 zucchini, chopped
2 cups (3¼ oz/90 g) baby spinach
4 cups (35 fl oz/1 liter) almond or rice milk
1 tablespoon (20 ml) lime juice
Celtic sea salt and freshly cracked black pepper, to taste
handful of fresh cilantro leaves, roughly chopped, to serve

Note: Pittas should omit the apple cider vinegar

SAFFRON AND SQUASH SOUP
SERVES 4–6

It's warm outside but you're still craving a sweet, comforting dish. Know the feeling?
Vatas and pittas, take a swan dive into this tasty soup and enjoy the creaminess of the
coconut milk and sweetness of the butternut squash. I've infused this summer soup
with saffron, as it's a refrigerant for the mind, helping to cool down thinking and clear
any anxious or worrisome thoughts.

2¼ oz (60 g) organic unsalted butter
    or ghee
1 leek, white part only, sliced
pinch of saffron threads
2 tablespoons (40 ml) apple cider vinegar
2 lb (900 g) butternut squash, peeled,
    seeded and chopped
2 carrots, diced
4 cups (35 fl oz/1 liter) chicken
    or vegetable stock
    (preferably homemade)
⅛ teaspoon ground cinnamon
⅛ teaspoon freshly grated nutmeg
¼ cup (2 fl oz/60 ml) additive-free
    coconut milk
pinch of Celtic sea salt
¼ teaspoon freshly cracked black pepper
microherbs, to garnish (optional)

Melt the butter or ghee in a large saucepan over medium heat.
Add the leek and saffron, and cook for 5 minutes or until the
leek is tender. Add the apple cider vinegar, squash, carrot, stock
and spices, then bring to a boil. Reduce the heat and simmer,
uncovered, for 20 minutes or until the squash and carrot are
tender.

Remove from the heat and cool slightly, then transfer to
a blender or food processor and process until smooth.

Return the soup to the pan and reheat gently. Divide among
serving dishes, then swirl through the coconut milk and season
with salt and pepper. Scatter over microherbs (if using) and
serve immediately.

P ▲ B ▲ P ▲ A ▲ Sw ▲ Sa ▲ So

CALMING CUCUMBER AND COCONUT SOUP
SERVES 6 (SMALL SERVINGS)

Fiery pittas need cooling blends. This refreshing, moisturising and soothing cold soup will help mellow the summer heat while giving your skin a subtle glow. Try it when you're feeling hot, bothered or angry, and enjoy an immediate calming effect on your mind and throughout your body.

2 Lebanese (short) cucumbers, peeled, seeds removed, and chopped
2 cups (17 fl oz/500 ml) additive-free coconut milk
¼ cup (¼ oz/7 g) cilantro leaves
grated zest of 1 lime
juice of 2 limes
¼ teaspoon ground cumin
Celtic sea salt, to taste

Place all the ingredients in a blender, reserving a little cucumber and cilantro to serve, and blend until smooth.

Chill well before serving topped with the reserved cucumber and cilantro.

K ▲ B ▲ P ▲ ▲ A ▲ Sw ▲ Sa ▲ So

Use only 1 teaspoon ghee

To balance vata, omit the pepper and replace the eggplant with butternut squash

To balance pitta, replace the eggplant with butternut squash

Note: All doshas should eat tomato only in moderation

ENERGIZING VEGETABLE STEW
SERVES 2–3

Heat the ghee in a wok or frying pan over medium–high heat. Add the cumin and mustard seeds and fry for 1 minute or until fragrant. Reduce the heat to medium. Add the garlic and ginger, and cook for 1 minute. Add the onion and chili, and stir-fry for 2–3 minutes or until the onion is translucent.

Add the vegetables, garam masala and turmeric, and stir to combine. Reduce the heat to low–medium and cook, covered, for 10 minutes. Remove the lid and cook for another 10 minutes. (Add a little filtered water during cooking if necessary to stop the vegetables drying out.) Season with salt.

Serve with brown rice crepes and cilantro and mint chutney on the side.

2 tablespoons ghee
1 teaspoon cumin seeds
½ teaspoon black mustard seeds
4 garlic cloves, grated
1 inch (2.5 cm) piece of ginger, peeled and grated
2 onions, diced
1 green chili, seeded and finely chopped
1 red pepper, diced
2 small zucchini, diced
1 small eggplant, cut into ½ inch (1 cm) dice
4 tomatoes, chopped
2 teaspoons garam masala
1 teaspoon ground turmeric
filtered water, as needed (optional)
Celtic sea salt, to taste
Brown rice crepes (page 243) and Cilantro and mint chutney (page 237), to serve

P ▲ B ▲ P ▲ A ▲ Sw ▲ Sa ▲ So

Omit the almond butter and use only 1 teaspoon ghee
To balance vata, use chai tea bags and omit the mint and parsley
To balance kapha, omit the almond butter

TEA-POACHED CHICKEN WITH GREEN BEANS
SERVES 4

Combine the water, tea bags, lemongrass, ginger, lime zest and mint leaves in a large saucepan over medium heat and bring to a boil. Cover, turn off the heat, and set aside for 10 minutes. Strain, discarding the solids.

Return the tea to the saucepan over medium heat. Bring to a boil then add the chicken breasts. Reduce the heat to low and simmer for 9–12 minutes or until just cooked.

Remove the chicken from the tea, reserving ¼ cup (2 fl oz/60 ml) of the tea, and slice the chicken into long, thin pieces. Set aside.

Combine the lime juice, vinegar, almond butter and the reserved tea in a bowl and whisk well.

Melt the ghee in a medium frying pan over medium heat. Add the garlic and fry for 1–2 minutes. Add the beans and pour over the tea mixture. Cook for 5–6 minutes or until the beans start to soften.

Transfer the chicken to a serving plate, top with the green beans and sauce, garnish with the parsley, season with pepper and sprinkle over the sesame seeds.

8 cups (68 fl oz/2 liters) filtered water
4 tea bags of your choice
1 lemongrass stem
1 inch (2.5 cm) piece of ginger, peeled and grated
1 tablespoon grated lime zest
3–4 mint leaves
4 boneless, skinless chicken breasts
1 tablespoon (20 ml) lime juice
1 tablespoon (20 ml) apple cider vinegar
¾ oz (20 g) almond butter
1 tablespoon ghee
4 garlic cloves, crushed
9 oz (250 g) green beans, trimmed and cut into 1 inch (2.5 cm) pieces
flat-leaf (Italian) parsley leaves, to serve
freshly cracked black pepper, to taste
2 tablespoons sesame seeds

V **K** ▲ B ▲ P ▲ A ▲ Sw ▲ Sa ▲ So

To balance pitta, replace the rosemary with mint and reduce the quantities of the spices

BAKED FISH WITH FLAXSEED CRUST
SERVES 4

Turn a simple fish fillet into a crispy yet moist and flavorful delight covered with a special crunchy flaxseed crust. Flaxseeds are an excellent source of omega-3 fatty acids and will help to lubricate vatas' dry intestinal tract.

4 rainbow trout fillets, bones removed
2 tablespoons ghee, melted
½ cup (1¾ oz/50 g) flaxseed meal
1 teaspoon dried rosemary
½ teaspoon Celtic sea salt
freshly cracked black pepper, to taste
Coconut brown rice with ginger and black sesame seeds (page 216) and Cilantro and mint chutney (page 237), to serve
lime halves, to serve

Preheat the oven to 345°F (175°C/gas mark 4) and line a baking sheet with parchment paper.

Place the fish skin side down on the prepared baking sheet and brush with the ghee. Combine the flaxseed meal, rosemary, salt and pepper in a small bowl, then spoon the mixture over the fish and press it down gently.

Bake for 25–30 minutes or until the crust is golden brown.

Serve on coconut brown rice with cilantro and mint chutney on top and lime halves on the side.

V K ▲B ▲P ▲A ▲Sw ▲Sa ▲So

Note: All doshas should eat tomato only in moderation

GREEN PEA CURRY
SERVES 3–4

Put the split peas and water in a medium saucepan and bring to a boil over medium heat. Reduce the heat to low and simmer, covered, for 30 minutes or until cooked. Strain the peas, reserving the liquid, and set aside.

Heat half the ghee in a large frying pan over medium heat. Add the onion, ginger, garlic and chili, and cook for 5–7 minutes or until the onion is golden. Add the turmeric, coriander and fennel seeds, and cook for 2–3 minutes. Add the tomato and cook for 5 minutes or until softened. Remove from the heat and allow to cool slightly, then place in a blender with ¼ cup (2 fl oz/60 ml) of the reserved pea liquid and blend to a paste.

Heat the remaining ghee in a large frying pan over medium heat. Add the garam masala and curry leaves, and cook for 1 minute. Pour in 1 cup (9 fl oz/250 ml) of the reserved pea liquid and bring to a boil. Stir in the cooked peas and spicy paste, then add the milk and warm through. Season with salt.

Garnish with extra curry leaves and serve with Indian dosas.

1½ cups (11½ oz/330 g) green split peas, soaked overnight in filtered water then rinsed well
6 cups (52 fl oz/ 1.5 liters) filtered water
2 tablespoons ghee
2 onions, diced
2 teaspoons freshly grated ginger
3 garlic cloves, chopped
2 green chilies, seeded and chopped
½ teaspoon ground turmeric
1 tablespoon ground coriander
2½ teaspoons fennel seeds
1 tomato, diced
1 teaspoon garam masala
6 curry leaves, plus extra to serve
1¼ cups (10¾ fl oz/310 ml) additive-free rice milk (kapha) or coconut milk (vata)
Celtic sea salt, to taste
Indian dosas (page 240), to serve

V K B ▲ P ▲ A ▲ Sw ▲ Sa ▲ So

To balance pitta, omit the chilies and garlic, and replace the brown rice flour with almond meal
or tapioca flour

CRUMBED FISH WITH SAUTÉED BEANS
SERVES 4

This is my friend and fellow author Erica Luiz's favorite Anglo–Indian-inspired dinner
dish, which she often cooks for her family. When we travelled to India together, she
introduced me to a myriad of tasty dishes in her hometown of Kochi.

5½ oz (4 ×150 g) white fish fillets,
    skin on
1 cup (5¾ oz/160 g) brown rice flour
1 teaspoon ghee
Coconut relish (vata; page 237) or
    Cilantro and mint chutney (kapha;
    page 237), to serve

HERB PASTE
1 cup (1 oz/30 g) cilantro leaves
½ cup (¼ oz/10 g) mint leaves
½ cup (1 oz/30 g) coconut flakes
1 green chili, seeded
1 inch (2.5 cm) piece of ginger, peeled
3 garlic cloves, peeled
1 teaspoon Himalayan salt
pinch of ground white pepper

SAUTÉED BEANS
1 cup (3¼ oz/90 g) additive-free
    desiccated coconut
½ cup (2½ oz/75 g) pepitas
    (pumpkin seeds)
½ cup (2½ oz/75 g) sesame seeds
1 tablespoon ghee
1 lb 2 oz (500 g) green beans, trimmed
    and steamed or boiled

To make the herb paste, process all the ingredients in a food
processor to form a thick paste.

Lay the fish on the counter, skin side down, and cover the
top with the paste, using a spatula to spread it evenly.

Place the flour in a bowl. Dip the fillets in the flour, coating
both sides. Cover and refrigerate until required.

Heat the ghee in a frying pan over medium heat. Cook
the fish in the hot pan, skin side down, for 2–3 minutes or
until golden, then turn carefully and cook the other side for
2–5 minutes or until cooked through (the cooking time will
depend on the thickness of the fillets.)

While the fish is cooking, prepare the sautéed beans.
Combine all the ingredients except the beans in a frying
pan over medium heat and cook, stirring frequently, for
4–5 minutes or until toasted. Scatter over the beans and
toss through.

Serve the fish with the beans, and with coconut relish (vata)
or cilantro and mint chutney (kapha) on the side.

P K ▲ B ▲ Sw ▲ So

ALOE VERA JELLY
SERVES 4

This refreshing detoxifying summertime dessert is the perfect vehicle for the soothing properties of aloe vera, to decongest the lymphatic system and eliminate pitta-aggravating impurities. It also cleanses and refreshes the digestive system. The hydrating powers of aloe heal the skin from within and promote the growth of collagen, while its bitter–cool quality is perfect for balancing a kapha-rich diet. This healthy, all-natural, delicious jelly is a delight for children as well as adults.

Heat the aloe vera juice in a medium saucepan over low heat. Add the agar agar and whisk until it dissolves. Add the lime juice and stevia, then continue to whisk until the mixture comes to the boil.

Remove from the heat and add the mint and lime zest. Pour into four serving dishes and refrigerate for 1 hour or until set.

3 cups (26 fl oz/750 ml) unsweetened aloe vera juice
⅛ oz (3 g) agar agar powder
1 tablespoon (20 ml) lime juice
6 drops liquid stevia
½ cup (1 oz/25 g) chopped mint
1 teaspoon grated lime zest

COCONUT BARK WITH ROSEWATER, PISTACHIOS AND RASPBERRIES
SERVES 4

2 oz (55 g) coconut butter
14 fl oz (v) can additive-free
    coconut cream
2 tablespoons (40 ml) rosewater, optional
    (page 127 or purchased)
pinch of Celtic sea salt
1 teaspoon alcohol-free vanilla extract
handful of raspberries
handful of pistachio kernels,
    roughly chopped

Line a baking sheet with parchment paper.

Melt the coconut butter in a bowl sitting over (but not touching) boiling water. Add the coconut cream, rosewater (if using), salt and vanilla, and stir to combine.

Pour onto the prepared sheet and scatter over the raspberries and pistachios.

Freeze for at least 30 minutes or until solid. Remove from the freezer and break into shards or chop into squares. Store in an airtight container in the freezer.

Note: Pittas should use egg white only and vatas should omit the lime zest; both should eat cashews only in moderation

SAFFRON AND COCONUT TAPIOCA PUDDING
SERVES 2–3

2½ cups (21½ fl oz/625 ml) additive-free
    coconut milk
¼ cup (3¼ oz/90 g) rice malt syrup
1 egg
½ cup (2½ oz/75 g) tapioca,
    washed, drained, then set aside
    for 15 minutes to soften and swell
    without being sticky
1 teaspoon grated lemon zest
¼ teaspoon saffron threads
1 teaspoon alcohol-free vanilla extract
½ cup (1¼ oz/35 g) shredded coconut
10 cashews
2 teaspoons extra virgin coconut oil

Combine the coconut milk and rice malt syrup in a medium saucepan over medium heat. Add the egg, whisking constantly until frothy. Add the tapioca, lemon zest, saffron and vanilla, then stir until the mixture comes to a boil. Stir constantly for 1–2 minutes, then reduce the heat to low and cook for another 10 minutes or until the tapioca is cooked through. Stir in 1 tablespoon of the shredded coconut. Pour into serving bowls.

Place the cashews and coconut oil in a small frying pan over medium heat and cook, stirring frequently, for 2–3 minutes or until the cashews are toasted. Remove the cashews from the pan, then add the remaining shredded coconut and cook, stirring constantly, for 1–2 minutes or until toasted.

Scatter the toasted cashews and coconut over the puddings. Serve immediately or refrigerate and serve chilled.

Note: Kaphas should eat chia seeds only in moderation

CHERRY CHOCOLATE OVERNIGHT PUDDING
SERVES 1

¼ cup (1¼ oz/35 g) chia seeds
1 cup (9 fl oz/250 ml) rice milk
1 tablespoon cacao powder
1 heaping teaspoon rice malt syrup
1 teaspoon vanilla powder or
    alcohol-free vanilla extract
6 fresh cherries, pitted and chopped,
    to serve
1 tablespoon cacao nibs, to serve

Combine all the ingredients except the cherries and cacao nibs in a small bowl. Cover and refrigerate overnight.

Serve topped with the cherries and cacao nibs.

V ▲ P ▲ A ▲ Sw ▲ So

To balance pitta, replace the orange juice with lime juice

To balance kapha, omit the coconut flakes and almonds, and use only half the coconut butter

RHUBARB AND STRAWBERRY CRUMBLE
SERVES 4

Preheat the oven to 400°F (200°C/gas mark 6) and line a small baking sheet with parchment paper.

Combine the rhubarb, strawberries, apple, orange juice, ginger and cinnamon in a medium saucepan over medium heat. Bring to a simmer and cook for 12 minutes or until the fruit is cooked.

Combine all the crumble ingredients in a small bowl and stir well. Spread over the prepared baking sheet and bake for 15 minutes or until golden, stirring occasionally.

Transfer the stewed fruit to a 8 inch (20 cm) square ovenproof dish, then spoon over the crumble and scatter the coconut flakes on top.

Bake for 10 minutes or until crispy on top.

1 bunch (1 lb 7 oz/600 g) rhubarb, roughly chopped
6 strawberries, hulled and sliced
1 apple, cored and sliced
¼ cup (2 fl oz/60 ml) freshly squeezed orange juice
1 inch (2.5 cm) piece of ginger, peeled and grated
1 cinnamon stick
¼ cup (½ oz/15 g) unsweetened coconut flakes

CRUMBLE
1 cup (3¼ oz/95 g) gluten-free rolled oats
¼ cup (1¼ oz/35 g) walnuts, roughly chopped
¼ cup (1¼ oz/35 g) slivered almonds
2 tablespoons pepitas (pumpkin seeds)
1 teaspoon ground cinnamon
½ teaspoon alcohol-free vanilla extract or vanilla powder
1¼ oz (35 g) coconut butter, melted

Autumn

Autumn is a time for rich culinary infusions of warming and flavorful meals, and as the weather cools down, an innate hankering for comfort food envelops us. Autumnal recipes are bursting with flavors and calming ingredients.

Try a Vata-calming Fig and Almond Butter Whip, and satisfy all your tastebuds with fulfilling Bircher Muesli. Indulge in hearty Spinach Pancakes, or nibble on Broccoli Bhajis or Sweet Potato Hash.

All the doshas are covered here with my dosha-taming soups. Ease yourself into autumn with my Traditional Lamb Korma or Fragrant Fish Stew, and then indulge your sweet tooth with Stewed Apple with Cloves or a delicious Pomegranate and Lime Cheesecake.

Note: Kaphas should replace the rice malt syrup with 6 drops liquid stevia; all doshas should drink this in moderation

HOLY BASIL COFFEE
SERVES 2

Sip on a cup of Ayurvedic coffee to improve digestion and reduce mucus within the body. Sacred basil is native to India and revered by Hindus – you will often see it planted around shrines. Holy basil seeds can be purchased online and can be grown easily in a container in your herb garden or on a windowsill. The plant has long purple flowers and green leaves with a clove-like fragrance. The leaves can be used for herbal teas, this coffee or added to salads.

Bring the water to a boil in a small saucepan. Add the cilantro and ginger, reduce the heat to low and simmer for 1 minute. Add the rice malt syrup and stir to combine.

Rub the basil between your hands to release the flavor, then add to the saucepan. Simmer for 2–3 minutes. Remove from the heat and leave to steep for 5 minutes, then strain (if preferred) and serve in glass, earthenware or ceramic vessels.

2 cups (17 fl oz/500 ml) filtered water
1 teaspoon chopped cilantro leaves
1 teaspoon ground ginger or dried ginger
1 tablespoon (20 ml) rice malt syrup
handful of holy basil

To balance kapha, replace the carrots with 3–4 celery stalks

LIME, MINT AND CARROT ZINGER
SERVES 1

6 carrots
6 mint leaves
½ inch (1 cm) piece of ginger, peeled
juice of 1 lime
4 ice cubes (optional)

Run the carrots, mint and ginger through a juicer, then add the lime juice. Transfer to a glass, add ice cubes (if using) and drink immediately.

VATA-CALMING FIG AND ALMOND BUTTER WHIP
SERVES 1

What's more comforting for vatas than the fragrant sweetness of figs and the creaminess of almond butter? This healthy treat tastes so indulgent, you'll hardly believe it's filling your body with grounded goodness or that it's a natural tonic, providing energy and vitality. Figs are cooling and soothing for the delicate tissues of the digestive system. This recipe is perfection on its own, but you can also use less almond milk and spread this sticky bundle of happiness on my Brown Rice Crepes (page 243).

1 cup (9 fl oz/250 ml) almond milk
4 figs
1 banana
¾ oz (20 g) almond butter

Process all the ingredients in a blender until smooth and creamy.

To balance vata, reduce the quantity of the cacao and replace the rice milk with almond milk
To balance pitta, use only the freshest yogurt, reduce the quantity of the cacao and replace the rice milk with almond milk

RAW CACAO SMOOTHIE
SERVES 1

Turning a chocolate milkshake into a good-for-you smoothie is simple – just use raw cacao. This substantial brekkie provides kaphas with many benefits, from antioxidants to stress-fighting magnesium, healing and relief from congestion. Sheep's milk yogurt is much easier to digest and creamier than cow's milk yogurt; it makes this luxurious glass of goodness double the fun and easier on the kapha constitution.

Process all the ingredients in a blender on high until smooth. If using cacao nibs, you can either blend them completely or leave some chunks. Garnish with extra cacao.

1 cup (9 fl oz/250 ml) rice milk
6 strawberries, hulled
½ cup (4½ oz/130 g) sheep's milk yogurt
1 tablespoon raw cacao powder or cacao nibs, plus extra to garnish

V   K   ▲ B ▲ P ▲ A ▲ Sw ▲ Sa ▲ So

To balance pitta, replace the brown rice flour with besan (chickpea), tapioca or amaranth flour,
replace the spinach with kale and use only a small quantity of salt

Note: All doshas can enjoy spinach in moderation

SPINACH PANCAKES
SERVES 2

Indians sometimes call pancakes eggless omelettes, and my spinach pancakes have all
of the flavor of pakoras or bhajis but with healthier ingredients. These flipping good
discs of nourishment are big on taste yet light on digestion-disturbing components.

1 cup (5¾ oz/160 g) brown rice flour
handful of cilantro leaves, roughly
    chopped
1 cup (9 fl oz/250 ml) almond milk
    (vata) or rice milk (kapha)
Celtic sea salt, to taste
2 tablespoons ghee
1 onion, finely chopped
2 garlic cloves, crushed
1 teaspoon freshly grated ginger
large handful of baby spinach leaves
freshly cracked black pepper, to taste

INDIAN-STYLE HUMMUS
14 oz (400 g) can chickpeas,
    rinsed and drained
2 tablespoons (40 ml) filtered water
2 tablespoons tahini
1½ tablespoon (30 ml) lemon juice
1 teaspoon lemon zest
1 tablespoon extra virgin
    coconut oil, melted
1 garlic clove, crushed
1 teaspoon curry powder
½ teaspoon ground cumin
½ teaspoon ground turmeric
Himalayan salt, to taste
extra virgin olive oil, for drizzling

Combine the flour and cilantro in a medium bowl. Gradually
add the milk, whisking until smooth (or use a blender if you
prefer). Season with salt. Set the batter aside for 15 minutes.

To make the Indian-style hummus, blend all the ingredients
except the salt and olive oil in a blender or food processor
until smooth. Season with salt, transfer to a serving bowl and
drizzle over the olive oil. (The hummus will keep in an airtight
container in the fridge for 3–4 days.)

Heat half the ghee in a medium frying pan over medium
heat, add the onion, garlic and ginger, and cook for 2–3 minutes
or until the onion is translucent. Add the spinach and cook
until it has wilted and the water has evaporated. Remove from
the heat, cool, then stir into the batter with a spoon, reserving
a little as a garnish.

Heat a large frying pan over medium heat and add a small
amount of the remaining ghee. Once the pan is hot, drop in
¼ cup (2 fl oz/60 ml) dollops of the mixture and cook until
bubbles form on the surface, then flip and cook the other side.
Transfer to a plate and keep warm. Repeat with the remaining
ghee and batter.

Divide between serving plates, then top with the hummus,
pepper and reserved spinach. Serve warm.

L–R: Fig, cardamom and quinoa bowl; Bircher muesli

To balance vata, replace the apple with 2¾ oz (80 g) coconut flakes and the apple juice with coconut water or almond milk

Note: Pittas and kaphas should eat sheep's milk yogurt only in moderation

BIRCHER MUESLI
SERVES 1

Combine the apple, oats, apple juice, yogurt and cinnamon in a bowl and stir well. Cover and refrigerate overnight (or if making the same morning, cover and refrigerate for 1 hour).

When ready to serve, stir through the seeds and flaxseed meal, and top with the blueberries. Serve with extra yogurt (if using).

1 apple, cored and grated
1 cup (3¼ oz/95 g) gluten-free rolled oats
½ cup (4 fl oz/125 ml) apple juice
½ cup (4½ oz/130 g) sheep's milk yogurt, plus extra to serve (optional)
2 pinches ground cinnamon
2 tablespoons pepitas (pumpkin seeds)
2 tablespoons sunflower seeds
2 tablespoons sesame seeds
1 teaspoon flaxseed meal
fresh blueberries, to serve

Note: Pittas should use only a small quantity of salt

To balance kapha, replace the almond milk with rice milk and the figs with 1 diced peach

FIG, CARDAMOM AND QUINOA BOWL
SERVES 2

Combine all the ingredients except the figs and coconut flakes in a small, heavy-based saucepan over medium heat and bring to a boil. Reduce the heat to low and simmer, covered, for 15–20 minutes or until the quinoa has absorbed the liquid.

Remove from the heat and allow to cool slightly, then fluff with a fork. Spoon into two bowls, top with the figs and coconut, and serve with extra milk (if desired).

½ cup (3½ oz/100 g) quinoa, rinsed and drained
¾ cup (6 fl oz/185 ml) almond milk, plus extra to serve (optional)
½ cup (4 fl oz/125 ml) filtered water
½ teaspoon alcohol-free vanilla extract
¼ teaspoon Celtic sea salt
¼ teaspoon ground cardamom
2–3 ripe figs, diced
⅓ cup (¾ oz/20 g) coconut flakes, toasted

V ▲ B ▲ P ▲ A ▲ Sw ▲ Sa ▲ So

To balance pitta, use only one garlic clove and omit the parsley; pittas should eat eggs and goat's cheese only in moderation

AVOCADO AND GOAT'S CHEESE ON CARROT AND ZUCCHINI LOAF
SERVES 4

While most breads are just full of empty promises and calories, this delicious loaf is packed with vitamins and nutrients to eat right for your shape. Generously endowed with vegetables, seeds, herbs and spices, it will soothe a vata's sensitive digestive system. Enjoy with smashed avocado, goat's cheese and a squeeze of lime for a delicious down-to-earth breakfast.

4 slices carrot and zucchini loaf
  (see below)
2 avocados, sliced
⅔ cup (2¾ oz/80 g) goat's cheese
1 lemon
extra virgin olive oil, for drizzling
  (optional)
freshly cracked black pepper, to taste

CARROT AND ZUCCHINI LOAF
(makes 1 loaf or 10 servings)
1 zucchini, grated
pinch of Celtic sea salt
1 large carrot, grated
2½ cups (9 oz/250 g) almond meal
¼ cup (1½ oz/40 g) sunflower seeds
2 garlic cloves, crushed
1 tablespoon nutritional yeast flakes
1 tablespoon chopped flat-leaf
  (Italian) parsley
½ teaspoon ground coriander
½ teaspoon ground cumin
1 teaspoon baking powder
2 eggs, lightly beaten
2 tablespoons ghee, melted

To make the carrot and zucchini loaf, preheat the oven to 350°F (180°C/gas mark 4) and grease a 8 inch × 3½ inch × 2½ inch (20 cm × 9 cm × 6 cm) loaf pan.

Place the zucchini in a sieve resting over a bowl. Sprinkle with the salt and set aside to drain for 10 minutes. Squeeze the zucchini with your hands to extract any excess water, then transfer to a bowl. Add the carrot, almond meal, sunflower seeds, garlic, yeast flakes, parsley, spices and baking powder. Mix well, then add the eggs and ghee. Stir to combine.

Spoon into the prepared loaf pan and bake for 50 minutes or until a skewer inserted into the center comes out clean and the top is golden. Cool in the pan for 10 minutes then turn out onto a wire rack to cool.

Toast four carrot and zucchini loaf slices under the broiler. Top each slice with half an avocado, and a quarter of the goat's cheese. Add a squeeze of lemon, a drizzle of olive oil (if using) and some pepper, then serve immediately.

P △ B ▲ P △ A ▲ Sw ▲ So

BROCCOLI BHAJIS
SERVES 4

If you like traditional bhajis, give this healthier version a try. Broccoli is loaded with essential nutrients and has many therapeutic benefits, including detoxifying properties. It also fills and satisfies the tummy for a long time. Make broccoli bhajis your favorite dish for taming potentially fierce pittas.

Sift the flours, baking soda and salt into a medium bowl. Gradually add the water, stirring well to avoid lumps. The mixture should have a smooth, paste-like consistency.

Heat some coconut oil (1½ inches deep/about 4 cm) in a medium, heavy-based saucepan over medium–high heat. Once the oil is hot (a small broccoli floret should sizzle and float), working in batches, dip the broccoli florets in the batter to coat well. Drop into the pan and cook until crisp on all sides. Lay on paper towel to drain off any excess oil while you cook the next batch.

Serve warm with chia jam and carrot and beet raita.

2½ cups (10½ oz/300 g) besan (chickpea) flour
2 tablespoons brown rice flour
pinch of baking soda
Himalayan salt, to taste
2 cups (17 fl oz/500 ml) filtered water
extra virgin coconut oil, for shallow-frying
2 cups (4¼ oz/120 g) broccoli florets
Chia jam (page 235) and Carrot and beet raita (page 235), to serve

Note: Pittas should eat spices only in moderation

To balance vata, replace the cauliflower with zucchini

To balance kapha, omit the coconut milk

TURMERIC CAULIFLOWER AND PEAS

SERVES 3-4

2 tablespoons ghee

½ teaspoon cumin seeds

2 onions, sliced

3 garlic cloves, crushed

2 inch (5 cm) piece of ginger,
    peeled and chopped

2 black cardamom pods

1 tablespoon ground turmeric

2 teaspoons ground coriander

2 teaspoons ground cumin

⅓ cup (2½ fl oz/80 ml) additive-free
    coconut milk

1 cauliflower, chopped into florets

2½ cups (12½ oz /355 g) frozen peas

pinch of Celtic sea salt

large handful of cilantro leaves, to serve

Melt the ghee in a large frying pan over medium heat, then add the cumin seeds and cook, stirring continuously, for 1 minute. Add the onion, garlic and ginger, and cook for 3–4 minutes or until the onion is translucent.

Crush the cardamom pods with a heavy knife, add to the pan with the remaining spices and cook for 1 minute. Add the coconut milk and cauliflower, and stir to coat with the spices. Continue cooking for 6–8 minutes, stirring frequently. Stir through the peas then reduce the heat to low and cook, covered, for 5–6 minutes or until the cauliflower is tender. Season with salt.

Serve topped with cilantro.

To balance vata, replace the green apple with 1 avocado and the cranberries with
½ cup (3¼ oz/90 g) grapes

Note: Kapha should use half the quantity of the dressing and replace the rice malt syrup
with 6 drops liquid stevia

APPLE, CELERY AND SPICED PECAN SALAD
SERVES 2

Combine the celery, apple, cranberries and pecans or almonds in a serving bowl.

Put all the dressing ingredients in a glass jar, seal tightly and shake well to combine.

Pour the dressing over the salad just before serving.

5 celery stalks, thinly sliced
   on the diagonal
1 green apple, cored and thinly sliced
¼ cup (1½ oz/40 g) dried cranberries
2 tablespoons spiced pecans (kapha;
   page 139) or almonds (pitta)

DRESSING
¼ cup (2 fl oz/60 ml) extra virgin olive oil
2 tablespoons sugar-free mustard
2 tablespoons (40 ml) lime juice
1 tablespoon (20 ml) rice malt syrup
Celtic sea salt, to taste

V ▲ B ▲ P ▲ A ▲ Sw ▲ Sa ▲ So ▣

To balance pitta, omit the chili and reduce the quantities of the spices

To balance kapha, reduce the quantity of the ghee and replace the sultanas with ½ cup (2½ oz/75 g) dried cranberries

SWEET POTATO HASH
SERVES 3–4

This is my friend Kim's sweet little recipe. She blogs over at spiritedmama.com and is a master of Indian cooking. The sweetness of the rice malt syrup doesn't overpower the recipe but adds another level of intensity that is offset by the dosas and the salt.

filtered water, for boiling

1 lb 2 oz (500 g) orange sweet potato, peeled and cut into 2 inch (5 cm) pieces

1 tablespoon ghee

1 onion, thinly sliced into rings

1 green chili, seeded and thinly sliced (optional)

3 garlic cloves, chopped

1 teaspoon thinly sliced ginger

1 tablespoon cumin seeds

1 tablespoon cardamom seeds

1 tablespoon mustard seeds

5 star anise

½ cup (3 oz/85 g) sultanas (golden raisins)

½ cup (2½ oz/75 g) sunflower seeds

1 tablespoon rice malt syrup

pinch of Celtic sea salt

cilantro leaves, to serve (optional)

Indian dosas (page 240) and Coconut relish (optional; page 237), to serve

Bring a large saucepan of filtered water to the boil. Add the sweet potato and cook for 10 minutes or until just soft. Drain and set aside.

Melt the ghee in a large, heavy-based saucepan over medium heat. Add the onion, chili (if using), garlic and ginger, and cook for 2–3 minutes or until just soft. Add the spices and cook for 1–2 minutes or until fragrant. (Reduce the heat or add a little water if they start to burn.) Add the sweet potato, sultanas, sunflower seeds, rice malt syrup and salt. Reduce the heat to low and continue cooking for 5–6 minutes, stirring carefully, so as not to break up the sweet potato. If the mixture appears too dry, add a few teaspoons of filtered water.

Transfer to a serving dish, top with cilantro (if using) and serve with coconut relish or raita (see tip below) on top and dosas on the side.

>>> — *Supercharged tip* — ≪≪≪

Whip up a quick raita by combining yogurt, grated cucumber and sweet paprika.

Note: Pittas should reduce the quantities of the spices
To balance kapha, omit grated or shredded coconut

VEGETABLE THORAN
SERVES 4

2 tablespoons extra virgin coconut oil

1 tablespoon black mustard seeds

1 teaspoon cumin seeds

1 inch (2.5 cm) piece of ginger, peeled
   and grated

2 garlic cloves, chopped

1 tablespoon ground turmeric

8–10 curry leaves

1 green chili, seeded and
   chopped (optional)

1 lb 2 oz (500 g) green beans, very thinly
   sliced on the diagonal

large pinch of Celtic sea salt

½ teaspoon freshly cracked black pepper

4 carrots, finely grated

½ cup grated fresh coconut or
   shredded coconut

filtered water, as needed

cilantro leaves and lime wedges
   (optional), to serve

Heat the coconut oil in a medium saucepan over medium–high heat. Add the mustard seeds and fry until they pop. Add the cumin seeds and cook for 1 minute or until they darken. Add the ginger and garlic, and cook, stirring constantly, until fragrant. Add the turmeric, curry leaves and chili (if using), and cook for 1–2 minutes. Stir in the beans, salt and pepper, then cook for 2 minutes. Add the carrot and cook for another 2 minutes. Add the coconut and a little filtered water, then stir to combine. Reduce the heat to low and cook, covered, for 8–10 minutes or until the vegetables are very soft. Add more water as needed during cooking to ensure the mixture is not too dry and to create steam.

Serve topped with cilantro and with lime wedges for squeezing over (if desired).

CREAMY MUSHROOM SOUP
SERVES 4

An Ayurvedic remedy for insomnia, mineral-rich mushrooms have an earthiness to calm and ground pitta's fire and kapha's heaviness. They're considered tamasic in Ayurveda, meaning they make you sleepy. For extra nutritional enhancement, I've included lemon zest to assist with digestion and turmeric to provide powerful anti-inflammatory agents.

Heat the ghee in a large saucepan over medium heat, then add the onion and cook for 1 minute. Add the mushrooms and cook for 2–3 minutes. Add the stock and milk, bring to a boil, then stir for 2–3 minutes. Add the spices and lemon zest, then cook for another 2 minutes.

Season with salt and pepper, and serve immediately.

1 tablespoon ghee
1 onion, finely chopped
6¼ oz (180 g) mushrooms, finely chopped
2 cups (17 fl oz/500 ml) vegetable or chicken stock (preferably homemade)
1½ cups (13 fl oz/375 ml) rice milk
pinch of ground cumin
1 teaspoon ground turmeric
1 teaspoon grated lemon zest
Celtic sea salt and freshly cracked black pepper, to taste

To balance vata, replace the lentils with tur dhal

To balance pitta, omit the garlic and cayenne pepper; pittas should use spices and garlic only in moderation

Note: All doshas should eat tomato only in moderation

REPLENISHING RED LENTIL SOUP
SERVES 4

Heat the ghee in a large, heavy-based saucepan over medium heat. Add the onion, garlic and ginger, and cook for 5 minutes or until the onion is soft. Add the spices and stir for another minute or until fragrant. Add the lentils, tomato, stock and lemon slices, stirring to combine. Bring to a boil, then reduce the heat and simmer, covered, for 25 minutes or until the lentils are soft. Add the lemon zest and juice, season with salt, and cook for a further 1–2 minutes.

Top with parsley (if using), season with pepper and serve with extra lemon slices.

1 tablespoon ghee
1 onion, chopped
3 garlic cloves, crushed
1 tablespoon freshly grated ginger
2 teaspoons ground cumin
¼ teaspoon cayenne pepper
1 cup (7¼ oz/205 g) red lentils, rinsed
    and drained
4 large tomatoes, chopped
4 cups (35 fl oz/1 liter) chicken
    or vegetable stock
    (preferably homemade)
½ lemon, sliced, plus extra to serve
grated zest and juice of ½ lemon
Celtic sea salt, to taste
2 tablespoons chopped flat-leaf (Italian)
    parsley, to serve (optional)
freshly cracked black pepper, to serve

⇛ Supercharged tip ⇚

Soaking grains, lentils, nuts and seeds for 30–60 minutes in warm water helps make them easier to digest. You could also cook them with asafoetida to help prevent gas and bloating.

V P ▲ P ▲ A ▲ Sw ▲ Sa ▲ So

Halve the quantity of the ghee

DOUBLE-DOSHA-PACIFYING SOUP

SERVES 4

1 tablespoon ghee
1 small onion, finely chopped
½ teaspoon curry powder
½ teaspoon freshly grated ginger
2 leeks, white part only, chopped
2 carrots, chopped
1 rutabaga, diced
2 cups (9 oz/250 g) sliced green beans
1 small beet, peeled
    and chopped
2 zucchini, chopped
5 cups (44 fl oz/1.25 liters) vegetable or
    chicken stock (preferably homemade)
1 tablespoon (20 ml) lime juice
1½ oz (40 g) cilantro
    leaves, chopped
Celtic sea salt, to taste

Heat the ghee in a large saucepan over medium heat and cook the onion for 3–4 minutes or until translucent. Add the curry powder and ginger, and cook for 1 minute. Add the leek, carrot, rutabega, beans, beet and zucchini, and cook for 2–3 minutes. Add the stock and bring to a boil, then reduce the heat and simmer, covered, for 15 minutes or until the vegetables are cooked.

Remove from the heat, add the lime juice and scatter the cilantro on top. Season with salt and serve.

P K ▲ B ▲ P ▲ A ▲ Sw ▲ Sa ▲ So ⬤

Note: Pittas should reduce the quantities of the spices
To balance vata omit the chickpeas and replace the red lentils with yellow lentils

BUTTERNUT SQUASH CURRY
SERVES 6

This curry is best eaten in autumn, when it will comfort you through colder weather by releasing the sun's energy the squash have absorbed over the summer. Squash have mild diuretic properties, and so will help to drain excess fluid. Their cooling nature makes them an excellent liver tonic for overheated pittas.

Combine the spices in a small bowl.

Heat the ghee in a large, heavy-based saucepan over medium heat. Add the onion and cook for 3–4 minutes or until softened. Add the spices and ginger, and cook, stirring frequently, for 2–3 minutes to release the flavors. Add the lentils, squash and water, and bring to a boil. Reduce the heat to low and simmer, covered, for 20 minutes or until the lentils are cooked. Add the chickpeas, spinach, lemon zest and juice, and cilantro, then cook for another 2 minutes.

Serve hot, with flatbread and chia jam.

1 teaspoon ground coriander
1 teaspoon fennel seeds
1 teaspoon ground cumin
1 teaspoon ground turmeric
1 teaspoon garam masala
pinch of chili flakes
1 teaspoon ground cinnamon
1 tablespoon ghee
1 large onion, sliced
1 inch (2.5 cm) piece of ginger,
    peeled and grated
¾ cup (5½ oz/155 g) red lentils,
    soaked overnight and rinsed
½ butternut squash,
    peeled and chopped into
    ¾ inch (2 cm pieces)
3 cups (26 fl oz/750 ml) filtered water
14 oz (400 g) can chickpeas,
    drained and rinsed
3 handfuls of baby spinach
1 teaspoon grated lemon zest
juice of 1 lemon
2 tablespoons chopped cilantro leaves
Flatbread (page 241) and Chia jam
    (page 235), to serve

To balance vata, omit the lime zest and replace the rice milk with coconut milk
To balance pitta, omit the chilies, reduce the quantities of the spices and replace
the rice milk with coconut milk

FRAGRANT FISH STEW
SERVES 4

1 lb 10 oz (750 g) white fish fillets,
    roughly chopped
1 teaspoon ground turmeric
1 teaspoon ground cumin
Celtic sea salt, to taste
grated zest and juice of 1 lime
¼ cup (1¾ oz/50 g) ghee
1 onion, finely chopped
4 green chilies, seeded and
    finely chopped
4 garlic cloves, crushed
1 inch (2.5 cm) piece of ginger,
    peeled and finely grated
¼ teaspoon ground cardamom
10 curry leaves
1 teaspoon asafoetida
1 cup (9 fl oz/250 ml) rice milk
1 cup (9 fl oz/250 ml) fish or chicken
    stock (preferably homemade)
freshly cracked black pepper, to serve
cooked brown rice, to serve

Place the fish in a bowl and sprinkle over the turmeric, cumin and a little salt. Add the lime zest and pour over the lime juice. Cover and refrigerate for 1 hour.

Heat the ghee in a large frying pan over medium heat, then add the onion and cook for 3–4 minutes or until translucent. Add the chili, garlic and ginger, and cook for 2 minutes. Stir through the cardamom, curry leaves and asafoetida, then add the milk and stock. Bring to a boil, then reduce the heat to low–medium and simmer, covered, for 10 minutes. Reduce the heat to low, add the drained fish fillets and cook gently for 5 minutes or until just cooked.

Season with salt and pepper, and serve on brown rice.

Note: Pittas should reduce the quantities of the spices and omit the tamari; all doshas should eat tomato only in moderation

To balance kapha, omit the carrot and zucchini

SLOW-COOKED BALANCING VEGETABLES
SERVES 6

Combine all the ingredients except the peas and pilau in a slow cooker. Cover and cook on low for 8–9 hours. Add the peas 10 minutes before serving.

Serve with quinoa pilau.

4 parsnips, peeled and diced
1 large onion, chopped
2 garlic cloves, crushed
2 carrots, diced
2 zucchini, chopped
¾ cup (6 fl oz/185 ml) vegetable stock (preferably homemade)
14 oz (400 g) can additive-free diced tomatoes
2 tablespoons curry powder
2 teaspoons cumin seeds or ground cumin
2 tablespoons wheat-free tamari
1 teaspoon ground turmeric
½ teaspoon Celtic sea salt
1 lb 2 oz (500 g) frozen peas
Quinoa pilau (page 222), to serve

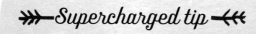

Supercharged tip

If you don't have a slow cooker, bake this in an ovenproof dish in a 275°F (140°C/gas mark 1) oven for 2–3 hours.

To balance pitta, omit the chili and reduce the quantities of the spices

TRADITIONAL LAMB KORMA
SERVES 4

¼ cup (1¾ oz/50 g) ghee
3 black cardamom pods, bruised
1 onion, finely chopped
2 garlic cloves, chopped
1 tablespoon freshly grated ginger
2 green chilies, seeded and
    finely chopped
1 tablespoon garam masala
2 tablespoons desiccated coconut
1 lb 12 oz (800 g) boneless lamb leg, diced
¼ cup (1 oz/25 g) almond flakes
2 tablespoons cashews, chopped
14 fl oz (400 ml) can additive-free
    coconut cream
filtered water, as needed
Celtic sea salt and freshly cracked
    black pepper, to taste
cooked brown rice or Flatbread
    (page 241) and Coconut relish
    (page 237), to serve

Heat the ghee in a large saucepan or wok over medium heat. Add the cardamom pods and cook for 30 seconds. Add the onion and garlic, and fry, stirring frequently, for 6–7 minutes or until golden. Stir in the ginger and chili, and cook for 2 minutes. Add the garam masala, coconut and lamb, and cook for 3–4 minutes or until the lamb is browned. Add the almond flakes, cashews and coconut cream. Reduce the heat to low, then cook, covered, for 45 minutes, adding filtered water during cooking if required.

Season with salt and pepper, then serve with brown rice or with flatbread on the side and coconut relish on top.

CHOCOLATE FUDGE
MAKES ABOUT 15 PIECES

This recipe is so easy to make, but it looks like you've gone to so much trouble. Even though the fudge appears to be iced, that's just the way it comes out!

Line a baking sheet with parchment paper.

Process the nut butter and coconut oil in a food processor until smooth. Add the remaining ingredients and process until smooth and creamy.

Spoon the mixture onto the prepared sheet to 1¼ inch (3 cm) thick and smooth the top with the back of a spoon or a spatula.

Freeze for at least 1 hour before slicing and serving. If stored for longer in the freezer you may need to transfer to the fridge to soften a little.

1 cup (9½ oz/270 g) almond butter
⅓ cup (2½ fl oz/80 ml) extra virgin coconut oil, melted
¼ cup (1 oz/30 g) cacao powder
¼ cup (3¼ oz/90 g) rice malt syrup
½ teaspoon Celtic sea salt
1 teaspoon alcohol-free vanilla extract

STEWED APPLE WITH CLOVES
SERVES 1

2 apples, peeled, cored and diced

1 tablespoon organic raisins (optional)

2 whole cloves

¼ teaspoon alcohol-free vanilla extract
    or vanilla powder

6 drops liquid stevia or ⅛ teaspoon
    stevia powder

¼ cup (2 fl oz/60 ml) filtered water

Churna masala for your dosha
    (page 238), for sprinkling

Combine all the ingredients except the churna masala in a small saucepan over medium heat and bring to a boil. Reduce the heat to low and cook, covered, for 20 minutes or until the apple is tender.

Sprinkle over your churna masala and serve warm.

P ▲P ▲A ▲Sw ▲So

Note: Pittas should eat cashews and pistachios only in moderation

POMEGRANATE AND LIME CHEESECAKE
SERVES 3–4

To make the base, pulse the cashews and shredded coconut in a food processor until finely chopped. Transfer to a large bowl and stir in the remaining ingredients. Turn out onto a clean work surface and knead to form a dough. Press the dough evenly into a 6¼ inch (16 cm) round cake pan, preferably springform, and freeze for 30 minutes.

To make the filling, process the pomegranate seeds in a food processor until liquefied. Strain and set aside.

Pulse the cashews in the food processor until finely chopped. Add the remaining ingredients and the pomegranate juice, and process until smooth.

Remove the cake pan from the freezer and spoon the filling onto the base, smoothing the top with a spatula.

Freeze for 45 minutes or until set.

To serve, remove the tin from the freezer and leave to stand for 20 minutes. Top with pistachios and reserved pomegranate seeds, then cut into wedges and serve.

½ cup (2½ oz/70 g) pistachio kernels, to serve

BASE

¾ cup (4¼ oz/120 g) cashews, soaked for 2 hours in filtered water, then rinsed and drained

1 cup (2¼ oz/65 g) shredded coconut

¼ teaspoon stevia powder or 12 drops liquid stevia

¼ cup (2 fl oz/60 ml) freshly squeezed lemon juice

1 tablespoon coconut butter, melted

FILLING

seeds of 2 pomegranates, 2 tablespoons reserved for garnish

3 cups (1 lb ½ oz/465 g) cashews, soaked for 2 hours in filtered water, then rinsed and drained

11½ oz (330 g) coconut butter

⅓ cup (2½ fl oz/80 ml) additive-free coconut milk

1 tablespoon grated lime zest

juice of 3 limes

1 teaspoon alcohol-free vanilla extract

2 teaspoons ground cinnamon

1 teaspoon ground cardamom

½ teaspoon ground allspice

Winter

Winter is the time to resurrect firm favorites, and winter warmers come in all shapes and sizes: stews, soups, one-pots and puds.

Take on a Breakfast Borscht or creamy Spiced Amaranth bowl. Cuddle up to Coconut Brown Rice with Ginger and Black Sesame Seeds or seasonal Squash Bake, and warm and tickle your insides with an Immune-boosting Soup.

Big meals, we have you covered – Tuna Tikka Curry ticks all the boxes, while One-pot Lamb and Swiss Chard means less time washing up and more time huddling up with cozy socks and a good read.

L-R: Pitta beauty brew;
Almond milk chai with
turmeric and fennel

To balance vata, omit the lavender and chamomile

To balance kapha, omit the licorice

PITTA BEAUTY BREW

SERVES 2

To prepare the tea mix, combine all the ingredients in a medium bowl. Transfer to an airtight container and store in a cool, dry place.

To prepare a brew, place the 1 tablespoon tea mix in a teapot. Bring the water to a boil and pour into the teapot. Infuse for 10–15 minutes then strain into mugs and add stevia and a lime wedge (if using).

Note: Licorice root can be purchased from health food stores or online.

1 tablespoon tea mix (see below)
2 cups (17 fl oz/500 ml) filtered water
stevia, to taste
lime wedges, to serve (optional)

TEA MIX
1 tablespoon lavender flowers
1 tablespoon dried mint
1 tablespoon fennel seeds
1 tablespoon chamomile flowers or tea
2 teaspoons licorice root or the contents of 2 licorice tea bags
½ teaspoon ground ginger

To balance pitta, omit the nutmeg and cloves

To balance kapha, replace the almond milk with rice milk

ALMOND MILK CHAI WITH TURMERIC AND FENNEL

SERVES 2

Place the tea bags and spices in a teapot.

Combine the almond milk and stevia in a medium saucepan over medium heat and bring to a boil. Pour into the teapot and infuse for 10 minutes.

Strain and serve.

2 decaf tea bags
1 cinnamon stick
½ teaspoon cardamom seeds
½ teaspoon fennel seeds
¼ teaspoon whole cloves
½ teaspoon ground turmeric
½ teaspoon ground ginger
¼ teaspoon freshly grated nutmeg
2 cups (17 fl oz/500 ml) almond milk
6 drops liquid stevia

TURMERIC, CARDAMOM AND CUMIN TEA
SERVES 1

¼ teaspoon ground turmeric
¼ teaspoon ground cardamom or
    the seeds from 2 pods, ground
¼ teaspoon ground cumin
1 cup (9 fl oz/250 ml) boiling
    filtered water
6 drops liquid stevia or ⅛ teaspoon
    stevia powder

Combine all the spices in a cup then pour in the boiling water. Infuse for 1 minute then add the stevia.

WEIGHT-REDUCING LEMON TEA
SERVES 1

This tea can be drunk upon rising and half an hour before meals, up to three times a day. The combination of apple cider vinegar and cayenne pepper gives your metabolism a boost and helps stimulate the digestive and fat-burning process.

1 tablespoon (20 ml) apple cider vinegar
pinch of cayenne pepper
6 drops liquid stevia
2 tablespoons lemon juice
1 cup (9 fl oz/250 ml) filtered water,
    boiled and cooled slightly

Combine all the ingredients except the water in a cup, then pour in the water. Stir gently to combine. Sip slowly.

Note: Kaphas should reduce the quantity of the sheep's milk yogurt

To balance vata, omit the mint

CILANTRO AND MINT LASSI
SERVES 2

Process all the ingredients in a blender on high speed until smooth. Pour into two glasses (strain if preferred).

1½ cups (13 fl oz/375 ml) filtered water

⅔ cup (6¾ oz/190 g) sheep's milk yogurt

3 mint leaves, torn

1 tablespoon chopped cilantro leaves

½ teaspoon freshly grated ginger

Celtic sea salt, to taste

6 drops liquid stevia (optional)

To balance pitta, replace the nutmeg with ground cinnamon and omit the ground cloves

SPICED AMARANTH
SERVES 2

Imagine cozying up on a crisp winter's morning with your hands wrapped around a comforting bowl of porridge. Amaranth is an easily digestible seed, and the addition of warming spices to this bowl of high-protein goodness makes it a flawless start to a vata's or kapha's picture-perfect day.

1 tablespoon ghee
1 inch (2.5 cm) piece of ginger,
   peeled and grated
1 teaspoon ground cinnamon
¼ teaspoon ground cardamom
pinch of freshly grated nutmeg
pinch of ground cloves
1 star anise
1½ cups (13 fl oz/375 ml) filtered water,
   plus extra as needed
pinch of Celtic sea salt
½ teaspoon alcohol-free vanilla
   extract or powder
¾ cup (5 oz/145 g) amaranth
¼ cup (1¾ oz/50 g) grated apple, to serve
milk of your choice, to serve (optional)

Heat the ghee in a medium saucepan over low–medium heat, then add the ginger and spices. Stir for 1–2 minutes or until fragrant. Add the water, salt and vanilla, then bring to a boil. Stir through the amaranth and return to a boil. Reduce the heat to low and cook, covered, for 20 minutes or until smooth and creamy. Add more water during cooking if needed.

Remove the star anise and serve with grated apple on top and your favorite milk poured over (if desired).

Use only 1 teaspoon ghee
To balance vata, omit the celery and turnip
To balance pitta, omit the garlic, celery, bay leaf, turnip, pepper and paprika

BREAKFAST BORSCHT

SERVES 4–5

This wonderful soup is no boring borscht experience, so start including it in your weekly winter repertoire. It's a beet-iful and bountiful way for kaphas to start the day and face the world brimming with boundless energy.

1 tablespoon ghee
2 garlic cloves, chopped
1 stalk celery, chopped
1 bay leaf
4 beets, peeled and roughly chopped
1 carrot, diced
1 turnip, peeled and diced
6 cups (52 fl oz/1.5 liters) vegetable
    stock (preferably homemade)
    or filtered water
3½ oz (100 g) kale, chopped
juice of ½ lemon
1 teaspoon Celtic sea salt
pinch of freshly cracked black pepper
pinch of sweet paprika
1 teaspoon chopped dill
flat-leaf (Italian) parsley, finely chopped,
    to serve

Heat the ghee in a large saucepan over medium heat. Add the garlic and celery, and cook, stirring frequently, for 2–3 minutes or until the celery has softened. Add the bay leaf, beets, carrot, turnip and stock. Bring to a boil, then reduce the heat and simmer, covered, for 30 minutes or until the vegetables are cooked. Add the kale and cook for another 10 minutes, then add the lemon juice, salt and pepper, paprika and dill.

Spoon into bowls and top with parsley.

P ▲ B ▲ P ▲ A ▲ Sw ▲ Sa ▲ So

INDIAN SPICED VEGETABLE PORRIDGE
SERVES 2

Combine the zucchini, spinach, carrot, spices, stevia, lemon zest and coconut milk in a small saucepan over medium heat and bring to a boil. Reduce the heat to low then add the almonds and simmer for 5 minutes.

Season with salt and serve topped with the walnuts.

½ cup (2½ oz/70 g) grated
  zucchini

1 cup (1½ oz/45 g) baby spinach,
  cut into thin strips
½ cup (2¾ oz/80 g) grated carrot
2 whole cloves
½ teaspoon ground ginger
½ teaspoon ground cinnamon
¼ teaspoon freshly grated nutmeg
¼ teaspoon stevia powder
1 teaspoon grated lemon zest
1 cup (9 fl oz/250 ml) additive-free
  coconut milk
½ cup (2¾ oz/80 g) chopped almonds
pinch of Celtic sea salt
¼ cup (1¼ oz/35 g) walnuts, chopped
  and toasted in a dry frying pan,
  to serve

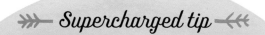

⋙ *Supercharged tip* ⋘

I like to pop the carrot and zucchini
in my food processor and process them
– it's a lot faster than grating by hand.

V ▲ B ▲ P ▲ A ▲ Sw ▲ So

To balance pitta, omit the watercress, apple cider vinegar and pepper, and replace the
walnuts with soaked almonds
To balance kapha, reduce the quantities of the goat's cheese and olive oil

GOAT'S CHEESE, FENNEL AND WALNUT SALAD
SERVES 6

It's quite possible to create a body-shaping and filling salad without hefty ingredients.
Pacify your vata tendencies with a fulfilling salad that combines creamy goat's cheese
and crunchy fennel with dry-roasted walnuts, giving you ample amounts of vitamin C,
phytonutrients and antioxidants. Fennel has a crispy and vivacious nature with a cool
quality to calm the mind and increase mental clarity. It's an excellent diuretic and can
help detoxify the blood, making it a wonderful preventative against bladder infections.

In a large bowl, toss together all the salad ingredients except
the salt and pepper.

Combine the dressing ingredients in a glass jar, seal tightly
and shake well. Pour over the salad and serve immediately,
sprinkled with salt and pepper.

1 romaine lettuce, leaves separated
2 cups (2¼ oz/60 g) watercress leaves
2 bulbs baby fennel, trimmed,
    thinly sliced
1¾ cups (7½ oz/210 g) goat's
    cheese, crumbled
½ cup (2½ oz/70 g) dry-roasted walnuts,
    coarsely chopped
Celtic sea salt and freshly cracked
    black pepper, to taste

DRESSING
⅓ cup (2½ fl oz/80 ml) extra
    virgin olive oil
2 tablespoons (40 ml) apple cider vinegar
2 tablespoons (40 ml) lemon juice
Celtic sea salt, to taste

K △ B ▲ P △ A △ Sw △ Sa △ So

To balance pitta, season only lightly, omit the cumin and replace the rice milk with coconut milk

Note: All doshas should eat spinach only in moderation

CUMIN CREAMED SPINACH
SERVES 4

This dish is so uncomplicated yet delicious. You can make it in about 10 minutes, but the creaminess of the rice milk, the subtle Indian influence of the spices and the nutritional goodness of the spinach provide a real wow factor. Serve it with quinoa or some protein and you have the perfect option for a weeknight when time is short and kapha is high.

2 tablespoons (40 ml) extra virgin
    olive oil or ghee
1 tablespoon tapioca flour
3 garlic cloves, crushed
8 cups (12¾ oz/360 g) baby spinach
⅔ cup (5½ fl oz/170 ml) rice milk
pinch of freshly grated nutmeg
¼ teaspoon ground cumin
Celtic sea salt and freshly cracked black
    pepper, to taste

Heat the olive oil in a large saucepan over medium heat. Slowly whisk in the tapioca flour and cook, stirring constantly, for 4–5 minutes. Add the garlic and cook for 1 minute. Add the spinach and cook, stirring frequently, until wilted. Stir through the milk, nutmeg and cumin, and cook for another 5 minutes.

Season with salt and pepper, and serve warm.

P K △ B ▲ P △ A ▲ Sw △ Sa △ So

Note: Pittas and kaphas can omit the garlic if they prefer
To balance vata, replace the kale with 1 diced avocado

BAKED SQUASH, QUINOA AND KALE
SERVES 4

Preheat the oven to 350°F (180°C/gas mark 4) and line a baking sheet with parchment paper.

Spread out the squash on the prepared baking sheet, pour over half the ghee and toss to coat. Bake for 30 minutes, turning occasionally. Remove from the oven and set aside.

Heat the remaining ghee in a medium saucepan over medium heat and cook the onion for 2–3 minutes or until translucent. Stir through the garlic, ginger, turmeric and ground coriander, then cook for 1 minute. Add the quinoa and water, bring to a gentle boil, then reduce the heat to low and simmer, covered, for 12–15 minutes or until all the liquid has been absorbed and the quinoa is cooked. Add the kale, squash and pepitas, and stir gently to combine.

Season with salt and serve topped with the cilantro leaves (if using), extra pepitas and a drizzle of lime juice.

1 lb 2 oz (500 g) squash,
    cut into thin wedges
2 tablespoons ghee, melted
1 onion, chopped
2 garlic cloves, crushed
1 teaspoon freshly grated ginger
1 teaspoon freshly grated turmeric
1 teaspoon ground coriander
1 cup (7 oz/200 g) quinoa, rinsed
    and drained
2 cups (17 fl oz/500 ml) filtered water
3–4 kale leaves, stems removed, chopped
¼ cup (1½ oz/40 g) pepitas (pumpkin
    seeds), toasted in a dry frying pan,
    plus extra to serve
Celtic sea salt, to taste
handful of cilantro leaves,
    to serve (optional)
freshly squeezed lime juice, to serve

V K ▲B ▲P ▲A ▲Sw ▲Sa ▲So

To balance pitta, replace the brown rice with quinoa, cooked according to the package directions (10–12 minutes)

COCONUT BROWN RICE WITH GINGER AND BLACK SESAME SEEDS
SERVES 2

Vatas and kaphas behold: this creamy, nutty rice is ideally enjoyed when you're craving warm, comforting food that captivates each and every one of your six tastes. The coconut milk gives a smooth, subtle, sweet taste to the brown rice that pairs very nicely with the shredded coconut and black sesame seeds. The ginger, mint and cilantro add a refreshing, light flavor and will aid digestion.

⅓ cup (2¼ oz/65 g) ghee
1 cup (7¾ oz/220 g) brown rice
1 cup (9 fl oz/250 ml) filtered water
1 cup (9 fl oz/250 ml) additive-free
    coconut milk (vata) or extra filtered
    water (kapha)
1 inch (2.5 cm) piece of ginger,
    peeled and sliced
1 teaspoon Celtic sea salt
2 garlic cloves, sliced
1½ tablespoons black sesame seeds,
    toasted in a dry frying pan
¼ cup (¾ oz/20 g) shredded coconut
small handful of cilantro leaves, to serve
small handful of mint leaves, to serve

Melt half the ghee in a medium saucepan over medium heat. Add the rice and stir to coat. Add the water, coconut milk or extra water, ginger and salt, then bring to a boil. Reduce the heat to low, then simmer, covered, for 45 minutes or until all the liquid has been absorbed.

Heat the remaining ghee in a separate medium saucepan over low heat and cook the garlic for 1–2 minutes. Add the sesame seeds and shredded coconut, and cook, stirring constantly, for 30 seconds.

Serve the rice topped with the garlic mixture, and the cilantro and mint.

V ▲ P ▲ A ▲ Sw ▲ Sa

To balance pitta, omit the cinnamon and use only a little salt

SQUASH BAKE
SERVES 3–4

Craving sweet food but not wanting to compromise when it comes to your health? This squash bake is just what you need to send energy downward and stabilize your vata fight or flight. This dish of warm, creamy goodness can be eaten as a side for dinner, or even for dessert! The naturally sweet taste of the squash is enhanced by the cinnamon and rice malt syrup, while the silkiness of the coconut cream and crunchiness of the pepitas (pumpkin seeds) make this no-nonsense bake even more decadent.

1 butternut squash, halved lengthwise, seeds and pulp removed
¼ cup (2 fl oz/60 ml) additive-free coconut cream
¼ cup (3¼ oz/90 g) rice malt syrup
¼ cup (1½ oz/40 g) pepitas (pumpkin seeds)
1 teaspoon ground cinnamon
¼ teaspoon Celtic sea salt

Preheat the oven to 345°F (175°C/gas mark 4).

Place the squash halves on a baking sheet, skin side up, and bake for 45–50 minutes or until cooked. Remove from the oven. When cool enough to handle, peel away the skin and discard. Transfer the flesh to a bowl and mash with a fork.

Reduce the oven temperature to 315°F (160°C/gas mark 2.5).

Add the remaining ingredients to the squash and mix well. Spoon into an ovenproof dish and bake for another 20 minutes.

Serve hot, straight from the oven.

Halve the quantity of the ghee and omit the coconut milk

CARROT AND GINGER SOUP

SERVES 4-6

Crush the coriander seeds with the mustard seeds using a mortar and pestle.

Heat the ghee in a large, heavy-based saucepan over medium heat. Add the onion and cook for 2–3 minutes, then add the ground spices, curry powder and ginger, and cook for 1–2 minutes or until fragrant. Add the carrot and stock, and bring to a boil. Reduce the heat to low and simmer, uncovered, for 25 minutes or until the carrot is tender.

Remove from the heat and allow to cool slightly. Purée in a blender or food processor – you may need to do this in batches.

Return the soup to the saucepan and add the coconut milk, and lime zest and juice. Reheat and season with salt.

Serve with a dollop of yogurt.

1 teaspoon coriander seeds
½ teaspoon yellow mustard seeds
2 tablespoons ghee
2 onions, chopped
½ teaspoon curry powder
1 tablespoon freshly grated ginger
4 carrots, thinly sliced into rounds
5 cups (44 fl oz/1.25 liters)
chicken or vegetable stock
(preferably homemade)
½ cup (4 fl oz/125 ml) additive-free
coconut milk
1½ teaspoons finely grated lime zest
1 tablespoon (20 ml) lime juice
Celtic sea salt, to taste
sheep's milk yogurt, to serve

L–R: Immune-boosting soup;
Ayurvedic weight-loss soup

P ▲ B ▲ P ▲ A ▲ Sw ▲ Sa ▲ So

Halve the quantity of the ghee

IMMUNE-BOOSTING SOUP
SERVES 3-4

Melt the coconut oil in a medium, heavy-based saucepan over medium heat. Add the onion and garlic, and cook for 3–4 minutes or until the onion is translucent. Add the remaining ingredients except the lemon juice and parsley and bring to a boil. Reduce the heat to low and simmer, covered, for 15 minutes or until the mushrooms are cooked through.

Remove from the heat, stir through the lemon juice, top with the parsley and serve.

1 tablespoon (20 ml) extra virgin coconut oil or ghee
1 small onion, chopped
6 garlic cloves, crushed
4 cups (35 fl oz/1 liter) vegetable stock (preferably homemade)
4 cups (9 oz/250 g) mixed mushrooms
1 carrot, grated or spiralized
¼ cup (1¾ oz/50 g) freshly grated ginger
grated zest of 1 lemon
pinch of Celtic sea salt
1 tablespoon (20 ml) lemon juice, to serve
¼ cup (⅛ oz/5 g) flat-leaf (Italian) parsley, to serve

V K ▲ B ▲ P ▲ A ▲ Sw

AYURVEDIC WEIGHT-LOSS SOUP
SERVES 3-4

My Ayurvedic cooking teacher, who is also an Ayurvedic doctor in India, swears by this soup to promote weight loss. Fenugreek helps improve digestion and reduce fatty tissue in the body. A wonderful herb with curative qualities, both its leaves and seeds can be consumed, the seeds whole or ground. The mucilaginous seeds are rich in dietary fiber, nutritious and soothing to the intestinal tract. Its flavor is similar to celery.

Bring the stock to a boil in a medium saucepan over medium heat. Stir in the remaining ingredients, reduce the heat to low and simmer for 10 minutes.

Spoon into serving bowls and top with extra pepper (if desired).

4 cups (35 fl oz/1 liter) chicken stock (preferably homemade)
8 curry leaves
1 teaspoon ground fenugreek
1 teaspoon ground ginger
freshly cracked black pepper, to taste

B ▲P ▲A ▲Sw ▲Sa ▲So

To balance kapha, omit the almonds and replace the coconut milk with coconut water

Note: All doshas should eat tomato only in moderation

QUINOA PILAU

SERVES 2–3

Quinoa is easy to prepare and to digest; a superfood with a nutty crunchiness. It contains more protein than most grains, more calcium than milk, and is rich in iron and magnesium. Slightly cooling and soothing to the digestive tract, this dish is a fantastic ally for aggravated vata and pitta.

2 tablespoons ghee
½ teaspoon yellow mustard seeds
½ teaspoon cumin seeds
8 curry leaves
¼ teaspoon fenugreek seeds
¼ onion, finely chopped
2 garlic cloves, chopped
1 large leek, white part only, chopped
2 green chilies, seeded and chopped
¼ teaspoon ground turmeric
1 red bell pepper,
   seeded and chopped
1 zucchini, chopped
2 tomatoes, chopped
14 fl oz (400 ml) can additive-free
   coconut milk
½ cup (4 fl oz/125 ml) filtered water
½ teaspoon garam masala
1 cup (7 oz/200 g) quinoa,
   rinsed and drained
2 tablespoons (40 ml) lemon juice
Celtic sea salt, to taste
½ cup (2¼ oz/65 g) slivered almonds,
   to serve
cilantro leaves, to serve

Heat the ghee in a large saucepan over medium heat, then add the mustard seeds and cumin seeds, and fry for 1 minute or until the mustard seeds pop. Add the curry leaves, fenugreek seeds, onion, garlic and leek, and stir-fry for 3–4 minutes, then stir through the chili and turmeric. Add the pepper, zucchini and tomato, and cook for 4–5 minutes or until the tomato starts to break down. Add the coconut milk, water and garam masala, and bring to a boil. Add the quinoa and lemon juice. Boil for 2–3 minutes, then reduce the heat to low and cook, covered, for 6–7 minutes or until all the liquid has been absorbed. Season with salt.

Remove from the heat and fluff with a fork. Serve topped with slivered almonds and cilantro.

⋙— Supercharged tip —⋘

Place a piece of paper towel between the saucepan and the lid in the very last stage, when the quinoa has absorbed all the liquid. It helps to soak up that last drop of moisture and make the quinoa very fluffy.

P **K** ▲ B ▲ P ▲ A ▲ Sw ▲ Sa ▲ So

Note: Pittas should omit the chili and use only moderate quantities of the spices
To balance vata, omit the Swiss chard or kale

ONE-POT LAMB AND SWISS CHARD
SERVES 4

Preheat the oven to 315°F (160°C/gas mark 2.5).

Heat the ghee in a flameproof, ovenproof dish over medium heat. Add the onion and garlic, and cook for 3–4 minutes or until the onion is translucent. Add the lamb and cook, stirring frequently, for 5–6 minutes or until browned. Add the spices and cook for another 3 minutes, then add the sweet potato and cook for another 3 minutes. Stir through the stock and dates, then cover and transfer to the oven for 1 hour or until the lamb is tender.

Add the Swiss chard and return to the oven for another 15 minutes. Season with salt and serve topped with the sunflower seeds (if using).

1 tablespoon ghee
1 onion, chopped
2 garlic cloves, sliced
1 lb 10 oz (750 g) boneless lamb leg, diced
1 teaspoon ground turmeric
1 teaspoon cumin seeds
1 teaspoon coriander seeds
pinch of chili flakes (optional)
1 sweet potato, peeled and diced
1½ cups (13 fl oz/375 ml) bone broth or chicken stock (preferably homemade)
2 dates, soaked in cold filtered water, drained and chopped
1 bunch (2 lb 4 oz/1 kg) Swiss chard or kale, stalks removed and leaves roughly torn
Celtic sea salt, to taste
¼ cup (1½ oz/40 g) sunflower seeds, toasted in a dry frying pan, to serve (optional)

Note: Kaphas should reduce the quantity of the yogurt; pittas should reduce the quantities of the spices and omit the chilies

TUNA TIKKA CURRY
SERVES 4

Be inspired by this lip-smacking tri-dosha dish, an antioxidant- and omega-3-rich meal that will melt in your mouth and satisfy and delight the whole family.

4 tuna steaks
ghee, for frying
salad leaves and Carrot and beet raita
    (page 235), to serve

MARINADE
1 cup (9¼ oz/260 g) sheep's milk yogurt
2 green chilies, seeded and chopped
handful of cilantro leaves, chopped
2 tablespoons (40 ml) lime juice
1 tablespoon crushed garlic
1 tablespoon freshly grated ginger
1 tablespoon (20 ml) mustard oil
1 teaspoon Celtic sea salt
¾ teaspoon ground turmeric
½ teaspoon garam masala
½ teaspoon freshly cracked black pepper
½ teaspoon cumin seeds, toasted in a dry
    frying pan

Rinse the fish, pat dry with paper towel and place in a large shallow dish.

Combine all the marinade ingredients in a blender. Add this mixture to the tuna and mix gently with a spoon to coat. Cover and refrigerate for 2 hours.

Heat a little ghee in a large frying pan over medium heat or on a barbecue hotplate and cook the tuna for 4–5 minutes on each side or until cooked to your liking.

Serve with salad leaves and carrot and beet raita.

V P ▲ B ▲ P ▲ A ▲ Sw ▲ Sa ▲ So ◉

MUNG BEAN DHAL
SERVES 4

2 tablespoons ghee
2 French shallots, thinly sliced
4 garlic cloves, sliced
1 tablespoon cumin seeds
1 teaspoon yellow mustard seeds
14 oz (400 g) yellow split mung beans
    (moong dal), soaked overnight in
    filtered water, rinsed and drained
filtered water, for boiling
1 inch (2.5 cm) piece of ginger,
    peeled and grated
1 tablespoon ground turmeric
2 green chilies, seeded and chopped
¼ teaspoon Himalayan salt
cilantro leaves, chopped,
    to serve

Heat the ghee in a small frying pan over medium heat. Add the shallots and garlic, and cook for 2–3 minutes or until golden. Remove from the pan and set aside. Return the pan to the heat and add the cumin seeds and mustard seeds. As soon as the mustard seeds start to pop, remove from the heat and set aside.

Place the mung beans in a medium saucepan and cover with filtered water. Bring to a boil over medium heat, skimming off any foam that comes to the top. Add the ginger, turmeric, chili and salt, then reduce the heat to low and simmer, partially covered, for 30 minutes or until cooked and creamy.

Transfer to serving bowls, add the reserved shallots, garlic and spices and top with the cilantro.

LEMON-INFUSED CARDAMOM BISCUITS

MAKES 14

My aromatic biscuits are infused with cardamom, an especially helpful spice for speeding up the digestive process. Enjoy them with a mint or chai tea.

Preheat the oven to 300°F (150°C/gas mark 2) and line a baking sheet with parchment paper.

Sift the flour, baking powder and ground cardamom into a medium bowl.

Combine the flaxseed meal and water in another bowl, then add the coconut sugar, coconut oil and lemon zest.

Add the flour mixture and combine with your hands to create a dough. Roll teaspoonfuls of the dough into balls and place them on the prepared baking sheet, flattening them with your palm. Leave a space between them, as they will spread during cooking.

Bake for 10–12 minutes, then cool on the tray.

1 cup (3½ oz/100 g) amaranth flour
½ teaspoon baking powder
3–4 cardamom pods, seeds removed and finely ground
1 tablespoon flaxseed meal
¼ cup (2 fl oz/60 ml) filtered water
⅓ cup (2 oz/55 g) coconut sugar or ⅓ cup (2¼ oz/60 g) xylitol
¼ cup (2 oz/60 ml) coconut oil, melted
1 teaspoon lemon zest

L–R: Spiced poached pears with orange; Chai crème brûlée

CHAI CRÈME BRÛLÉE
MAKES 4

Combine the coconut cream, almond milk, rice malt syrup, tea bag, spices and vanilla in a medium saucepan over medium heat. Bring to simmering point but do not allow to boil. Simmer for 5 minutes, stirring occasionally. Strain then return the liquid to the saucepan, discarding the solids.

Place the agar agar in a small bowl, and ladle over a little of the coconut mixture. Stir well, then slowly pour back into the saucepan, stirring well until dissolved. Pour into ramekins and refrigerate for 3–4 hours or until set.

When ready to serve, cover the top with an even layer of coconut sugar and place under the broiler set to high, or use a blowtorch, until a caramelized crust appears on top.

14 fl oz (400 ml) can additive-free coconut cream
½ cup (4 fl oz/125 ml) almond milk
1 tablespoon (20 ml) rice malt syrup
1 chai tea bag
½ cinnamon stick
6 whole cloves
4 cardamom pods, bruised
½ teaspoon alcohol-free vanilla extract
1 teaspoon agar agar
⅓ cup (2 oz/55 g) coconut sugar

SPICED POACHED PEARS WITH ORANGE
SERVES 2

Preheat the oven to 350°F (180°C/gas mark 4).

Arrange the pear halves in a small, 4 cup (35 fl oz/1 liter) capacity ovenproof dish. Combine the remaining ingredients except the walnuts in a bowl (retaining a few strips of orange zest to serve) and pour over the pears.

Bake for 30–40 minutes or until the pears are cooked through, turning them in the liquid halfway through.

Remove from the oven and top with the reserved orange zest. Drizzle with the reserved orange juice and top with the toasted walnuts (if using).

2 pears, peeled, cored (optional) and cut in half lengthwise
2 cups (17 fl oz/500 ml) rice milk
1 orange, zest cut into narrow strips, 2 tablespoons (40 ml) juice reserved to serve
3 whole cloves
½ teaspoon ground cinnamon
½ teaspoon vanilla powder
¼ cup (1¼ oz/35 g) walnuts, toasted in a dry frying pan and chopped (optional)

LEMONY COCONUT MOUSSE
SERVES 2

This refreshing and creamy coconut mousse is a true supporter for the thyroid, the master gland, which governs metabolism. In Ayurvedic medicine, an agitated liver should be moistened with good fats. Coconut replenishes a liver deficient in fats, and has special cooling properties to soothe an overheated liver, a problem that often befalls aggravated pittas.

14 fl oz (2 × 400 ml) cans additive-free coconut milk, chilled overnight in the fridge
2 tablespoons coconut sugar
½ teaspoon alcohol-free vanilla extract
grated zest of 1 lemon, plus extra to serve
pinch of Himalayan salt
caramelized lemon, to serve (optional)

Skim the cream from the top of the coconut milk and place in a small mixing bowl – you need 1 cup (9 fl oz/250 ml). (Reserve the remaining liquid in the bottom of the cans for use in smoothies.) Whip the cream using hand-held beaters on high for 2–3 minutes or until soft peaks form. Add the coconut sugar and vanilla, and continue beating for 1 minute. Gently fold in the lemon zest and salt.

Spoon the mixture into individual serving dishes and refrigerate until ready to serve. Top with extra lemon zest and caramelized lemon (if using), and serve.

>>> Supercharged tip <<<

Caramelize lemon slices in a hot, dry frying pan. You can add a little rice malt syrup, if you like.

Year-round staples

Breads, wraps and extras

Note: Kaphas should reduce the quantity of the chia seeds

CHIA JAM
SERVES 4

This natural, sugar-free jam suits all doshas. Fruit jams are delicious, but obtaining the desired consistency and firmness usually requires a large quantity of white sugar. This recipe uses chia seeds to create a perfect consistency, and rice malt syrup to add sweetness to the apple and berries. Delicious on its own, it can be used as a topping for pancakes – or a dollop added to the mixing bowl will sweeten up cakes, and a spoonful added to the pan will highlight curries.

Combine the apple, berries, water and rice malt syrup in a small, heavy-based saucepan over medium heat and bring to a boil. Reduce the heat to low and simmer for 20 minutes or until the consistency is thick.

Remove from the heat, stir through the chia seeds and transfer to a sterilized jar.

The jam will keep in the fridge for 5 days.

1 apple, cored and grated
1 cup (4½ oz/125 g) mixed berries
1 cup (9 fl oz/250 ml) filtered water
¼–⅓ cup (3¼–4¼ oz/90–120 g) rice malt syrup, to taste
¼ cup (1¼ oz/35 g) chia seeds

CARROT AND BEET RAITA
SERVES 3–4

Combine all the ingredients in a large bowl by mixing gently with a spoon.

The raita will keep in an airtight container in the fridge for 3–4 days.

2 cups (1 lb 2½ oz/520 g) sheep's milk yogurt
1 raw beet, peeled and grated
1 carrot, grated
1 onion, finely chopped
1 small bell pepper, finely chopped
1 garlic clove, crushed
1 teaspoon ground cardamom
Himalayan salt, to taste

L–R: Cilantro and mint chutney; Coconut relish

COCONUT RELISH
MAKES 1 CUP

Process all the ingredients except the salt in a food processor to your desired consistency, adding more filtered water if necessary. Season with salt.

The relish will keep in an airtight container in the fridge for 2 days.

½ small green chili, seeded and chopped
½ inch (1 cm) piece of ginger, chopped
1 cup (2¼ oz/65 g) shredded coconut
½ cup (4 fl oz/125 ml) filtered water,
    plus extra as needed
2 tablespoons (40 ml) lime juice
1 tablespoon chopped cilantro leaves
2 tablespoons ghee
½ teaspoon black mustard seeds
½ teaspoon cumin seeds
¼ teaspoon asafoetida
Celtic sea salt, to taste

To balance vata, omit the mint
To balance pitta, omit the chili

CILANTRO AND MINT CHUTNEY
SERVES 3–4

Combine all the ingredients in a blender until smooth, or to your desired consistency.

The chutney will keep in an airtight container in the fridge for 2 days.

2¼ oz (65 g) mint
2¾ oz (80 g) cilantro leaves
1 green chili, seeded
2 garlic cloves
2 tablespoons (40 ml) lime juice
1 tablespoon tamarind paste
½ teaspoon cumin seeds
6 drops liquid stevia
pinch of Celtic sea salt

CHURNA MASALAS: HERB AND SPICE BLENDS FOR COOKING

 VATA CHURNA MASALA

 B ▲ P ▲ A ▲ Sw ▲ Sa

MAKES ½ CUP

2 tablespoons fennel seeds
1 tablespoon coriander seeds
1 tablespoon cumin seeds
1 tablespoon ground turmeric
2 teaspoons ground ginger
2 teaspoons Himalayan salt
1 teaspoon asafoetida

 PITTA CHURNA MASALA

▲ B ▲ P ▲ A ▲ Sw

MAKES ½ CUP

2 tablespoons fennel seeds
2 tablespoons coriander seeds
2 tablespoons chopped mint
1 tablespoon cardamom seeds
½ teaspoon saffron threads
¼ teaspoon ground ginger

Ⓚ KAPHA CHURNA MASALA

▲ B ▲ P ▲ A ▲ Sw

MAKES ½ CUP

2 tablespoons coriander seeds
1 tablespoon cumin seeds
1 tablespoon fenugreek seeds
1 tablespoon ground ginger
1 tablespoon ground turmeric
1 tablespoon ground cinnamon
1 teaspoon ground cloves
¼ teaspoon freshly cracked
    black pepper
¼ teaspoon chili powder

Gently toast the spices for your dosha in a dry frying pan over medium heat until fragrant, then grind using a mortar and pestle. Store in an airtight container.

To balance pitta, omit the fenugreek

INDIAN DOSAS
MAKES 10

½ cup (3¾ oz/110 g) urad dal
1 teaspoon fenugreek seeds
pinch of Himalayan salt, plus extra
    to taste
1½ cups (7½ oz/210 g) quinoa flour
4 cups (35 fl oz/1 liter) filtered water,
    plus extra for soaking
ghee, for shallow-frying

Soak the urad dal and fenugreek overnight in a bowl of filtered water with the salt.

Rinse the dal, place in a blender with the flour and blend to a fine paste. Add enough of the water to make a thin batter. Pour into a large heatproof bowl.

Heat the oven on 400°F (200°C/gas mark 6) for 10 minutes, then turn the oven off. Sit the bowl in the oven for 15 minutes or until the batter is slightly bubbly and frothy. This traditional fermenting step is optional – the taste is the same whether you do it or not.) Remove from the oven and season with salt.

Heat a frying pan over high heat and add a small amount of ghee. Ladle about ⅓ cup (2½ fl oz/80 ml) batter into the pan and quickly swirl to spread evenly over the base of the pan. Add a few drops of ghee. When the edges are looking crisp, fold the dosa in half and remove from the pan. Repeat with the remaining batter.

FLATBREAD
MAKES 2

Flatbread works as an accompaniment for a festive dinner or barbecue, to soak up the brave flavors of your dishes. It's always a most welcome alternative to rice cakes and carrot sticks.

Preheat the oven to 345°F (175°C/gas mark 4).

Combine the almond meal, salt and baking powder in a large bowl. Add the olive oil, and rub it into the flour mixture with your fingertips until it resembles breadcrumbs. Stir in the egg and vinegar using a wooden spoon.

Turn the mixture out onto a lightly floured work surface. Roll it into a ball – it will feel quite sticky, but knead it for a few minutes until a smooth dough forms. Divide it in two and set aside for 5–10 minutes.

Cut out four pieces of parchment paper, approximately 8 inches × 8 inches (20 cm × 20 cm), and lay one piece out on the work surface. Transfer one portion of the the dough to the parchment paper and lay another piece of parchment paper on top. Using a rolling pin, roll out the dough to form a circle about 6 inches (15 cm) in diameter and about ½ inch (1 cm) thick. Repeat with the other portion of dough and the remaining pieces of parchment paper.

Gently peel off the top layers of parchment paper and lift the dough circles and the bottom layers of parchment paper onto a baking sheet. Transfer to the oven and bake for 12 minutes or until golden.

Remove from the oven and peel off the parchment paper – it should come away quite easily. Transfer the flatbreads to a wire rack to cool until crunchy.

1½ cups (5½ oz/150 g) almond meal
¼ teaspoon Celtic sea salt
¼ teaspoon gluten-free baking powder
1 tablespoon (20 ml) extra virgin olive oil
1 egg, lightly beaten
1 tablespoon apple cider vinegar
gluten-free plain (all-purpose) flour, for dusting

BROWN RICE CREPES
MAKES 6–8

My funky cool crepes perform the perfect duet, like a soul-shaking Bollywood couple on the eve of their wedding night. Fine crepes act as wraps to hold vegetables, scrambled egg or ground meat tightly; they also work as a grounding base for sweetened breakfasts and jammy desserts.

Combine the flour, baking powder and salt in a small bowl then set aside.

In a large bowl, whisk together the eggs and rice malt syrup, then add the dry ingredients and stir to combine. Add the milk gradually, whisking until smooth. Set the batter aside for 15 minutes.

Heat a little ghee in a frying pan over medium heat. Pour about ⅓ cup (2½ fl oz/80 ml) batter into the pan and swirl to spread evenly over the base of the pan. Cook until golden, then flip and cook the other side. Remove the crepe from the pan and lay on paper towel to drain off any excess oil. Repeat with the remaining batter.

1 cup (5¾ oz/160 g) brown rice flour
2 teaspoons baking powder
¼ teaspoon Celtic sea salt
2 eggs (vata) or egg whites (kapha)
2 tablespoons (40 ml) rice malt syrup
1 cup (9 fl oz/250 ml) rice milk (vata) or almond milk (kapha)
ghee, for shallow-frying

P ▲Sw ▲Sa

To balance kapha, replace the rice flour with brown rice flour

OM PUDI (CRISPY RIBBON BISCUITS)

1 heaping teaspoon ajwain (carom seeds)
filtered water, for soaking
3 cups (12¾ oz/360 g) besan
    (chickpea) flour
¼ cup (1½ oz/45 g) brown rice flour
Celtic sea salt, to taste
1 teaspoon ghee, melted
coconut oil, for deep-frying

Soak the ajwain in filtered water for 10–15 minutes. Drain, then grind using a mortar and pestle to make a paste. You may need to add a little filtered water.) Strain through a fine-mesh sieve, pressing the paste through with the base of a spoon.

Sift the besan flour, rice flour and salt onto a work surface. Make a well in the middle and then add the ajwain paste and ghee. Mix with your hands until soft and smooth, sprinkling with a little water if needed. Roll or press into a rough rectangle shape about ¼ inch (3 mm) thick. Cut into very fine strips that resemble pasta ribbons.

Heat some coconut oil (¾ inches deep/about 2 cm) in a heavy-based saucepan over medium heat. Working in batches, drop in the ribbons of dough and cook until crunchy. Remove from the oil using a slotted spoon or tongs and lay on paper towel to drain off any excess oil while you cook the next batch.

Store the cooled biscuits in an airtight container in a cool, dry place for 3–4 days.

⋙ Supercharged tip ⋘

Ajwain can be bought from specialist spice shops.

To balance kapha, replace the basmati rice with brown rice and cook the pilau for 40 minutes

SPICED BASMATI PILAU
SERVES 4–6

This is my lovely friend Cindy Luken's favorite recipe. She's been making it for 25 years and it's a part of her go-to repertoire – you know, those favorite dishes that you can make with your eyes closed and that you know everyone will love and that it will love you back? She has a lovely bunch of Indian recipes she rolls out when I come over for a quick fix. Try her Keema matar (page 118) or Tamatar Salat (page 139).

Rinse the rice under cold water until the water runs clear. Drain well and set aside.

Melt the ghee in a large, heavy-based saucepan over medium heat. Add the onion, cardamom pods, cloves and peppercorns, and cook, stirring frequently, for 6–7 minutes or until the onion is golden. Add the drained rice and fry for 5 minutes.

Pound the saffron with the boiling water using a mortar and pestle. Add to the rice with the stock and bring to a boil, then reduce the heat and cook, covered, for 20–25 minutes or until the liquid has been absorbed.

Remove the cardamom pods and cloves, and fluff up the rice with a fork.

Sprinkle over pistachios, pine nuts, almonds or sultanas (if using).

2½ cups (1 lb 2 oz/500 g) basmati rice
¼ cup (1¾ oz/50 g) ghee
1 large onion, finely diced
6 cardamom pods, bruised
6 whole cloves
1 teaspoon black peppercorns
½ teaspoon saffron threads
2 tablespoons boiling filtered water
30 fl oz (900 ml) chicken stock (preferably homemade)
1 teaspoon Himalayan salt
pistachio kernels, pine nuts, roughly chopped almonds or sultanas (golden raisins), to serve (optional)

Recipes for fasting

160 calories (670 kJ)

BREAKFAST: ORANGE CINNAMON PORRIDGE
SERVES 1

¾ cup (6 fl oz/185 ml) filtered water,
    plus extra for oats as needed
1 small orange, sliced
1 cinnamon stick
stevia, to taste
¼ cup (1 oz/25 g) gluten-free rolled oats
½ teaspoon ground cinnamon
½ teaspoon freshly grated nutmeg
½ teaspoon alcohol-free vanilla extract

Combine ¼ cup (2 fl oz/60 ml) of the water with the orange, cinnamon stick and stevia in a medium saucepan over high heat and bring to a boil. Reduce the heat to low and simmer, covered, for 10 minutes, adding a little more water during cooking if necessary.

Meanwhile, combine the oats, the remaining water and the spices and vanilla in a small saucepan. Bring to a boil, then reduce the heat to low and simmer, covered, for 10–15 minutes, stirring frequently, until the oats are cooked, adding more water during cooking if necessary.

Serve the oats topped with the stewed orange slices.

180 calories (750 kJ)

LUNCH: GREEN BEAN, RADISH AND AVOCADO SALAD
SERVES 1

7 oz (200 g) green beans,
    trimmed and sliced
¼ avocado, diced
5 radishes, thinly sliced
freshly cracked black pepper, to taste

VINAIGRETTE
2 tablespoons (40 ml) apple cider vinegar
1 teaspoon mustard
Himalayan salt and freshly cracked
    black pepper, to taste
stevia, to taste

Whisk all the vinaigrette ingredients together in a small bowl.

Steam the beans for 3–4 minutes or until al dente.

Combine the beans, avocado and radish in a serving bowl, drizzle with the vinaigrette and sprinkle over a little pepper.

V ▲ B ▲ P ▲ A ▲ Sw ▲ Sa ▲ So ◉

160 calories (670 kJ)

DINNER: LEMONGRASS CHICKEN WITH GRILLED ASPARAGUS
SERVES 1

Pat the chicken dry with paper towel. Using a sharp knife, make a slit in the chicken and push through the lemongrass stem.

Pound the lemongrass, garlic, ginger, lime juice and chili flakes in a mortar and pestle to make a paste. Rub all over the chicken and set aside on a baking sheet for 20–30 minutes.

Preheat the oven to 400°F (200°C/gas mark 6) and a chargrill pan to high.

Sear the chicken on the chargrill pan on both sides then transfer to a baking sheet. Roast the chicken, uncovered, for 10–15 minutes or until golden brown and cooked through.

Meanwhile, prepare the asparagus by drizzling the olive oil over the slices, ensuring they are completely coated. Season with salt. Cook the asparagus in the chargrill pan for 5 minutes, rolling each spear every minute. It should begin to brown in spots, but take care not to burn it.

Serve the chicken on the asparagus, seasoned to taste with salt and pepper.

3 oz (85 g) organic, boneless, skinless chicken breast (about half a breast)
1 lemongrass stem, trimmed
2 garlic cloves, crushed
½ teaspoon freshly grated ginger
1 teaspoon lime juice
pinch of chili flakes
Himalayan salt and freshly cracked black pepper, to taste

GRILLED ASPARAGUS
5 asparagus spears, sliced
1 teaspoon extra virgin olive oil
Celtic sea salt, to taste

Clockwise from top left: Lemongrass chicken with grilled asparagus; Green bean, radish and avocado salad; Orange cinnamon porridge

165 calories (690 kJ)

BREAKFAST: CHIA BREAKFAST BOWL
SERVES 1

¾ cup (6 fl oz/185 ml) filtered water
½ teaspoon alcohol-free vanilla extract
3 drops liquid stevia
1½ tablespoons chia seeds
¼ teaspoon ground cardamom
¼ teaspoon freshly grated nutmeg
¼ teaspoon ground cinnamon
5 almonds, roughly chopped, to serve

Place all the ingredients except the almonds in a bowl and stir to combine. Cover and refrigerate overnight to let the chia seeds absorb the liquid.

Serve topped with the almonds.

95 calories (400 kJ)

LUNCH: EGG-WHITE OMELETTE WITH ZUCCHINI AND MUSHROOMS
SERVES 1

1½ oz (45 g) mixed mushrooms,
    larger ones torn
1 small zucchini, grated
1 teaspoon ground cumin
½ teaspoon ground coriander
4 egg whites, lightly beaten
Himalayan salt and freshly cracked
    black pepper, to taste

Combine the mushrooms, zucchini and spices with a few drops of filtered water in a frying pan over medium heat and cook for 1 minute. Reduce the heat to low and add the egg whites, salt and pepper. Cover and cook for 5 minutes, or until the egg is cooked.

200 calories (840 kJ)

DINNER: GRILLED LEMON SHRIMP WITH CAULIFLOWER MASH

SERVES 1

To make the cauliflower mash, steam the cauliflower for 10 minutes or until soft. Transfer to a food processor with the stock and process until smooth. Stir in the nutritional yeast and season with salt and pepper.

To prepare the shrimp, combine all the ingredients in a bowl and set aside for 15 minutes. Heat a medium frying pan over medium heat. Add the shrimp with their marinade, and stir-fry for 5–8 minutes or until cooked through.

Serve the shrimp on top of the cauliflower mash, sprinkled with pepper and garnished with the micro cilantro.

freshly cracked black pepper, to taste
small handful of micro cilantro leaves,
    to serve

SHRIMP
5 raw shrimp, peeled and deveined, tails
    left intact
zest of 1 lemon
1 teaspoon extra virgin olive oil
a few cilantro sprigs
Himalayan salt and freshly cracked
    black pepper, to taste

CAULIFLOWER MASH
½ cauliflower, cut into large florets
½ cup (4 fl oz/125 ml) hot chicken stock
    (preferably homemade)
¼ cup (¾ oz/20 g) nutritional yeast flakes
Himalayan salt and freshly cracked black
    pepper, to taste

*Clockwise from top left:
Egg-white omelette with zucchini
and mushrooms; Grilled lemon
shrimp with cauliflower mash;
Chia breakfast bowl*

110 calories (460 kJ)

BREAKFAST: BAKED APPLE WITH PRUNES, CINNAMON AND CARDAMOM
SERVES 1

1 apple, cored but left whole
filtered water, for baking
½ teaspoon ground cinnamon
¼ teaspoon ground cardamom
¼ teaspoon freshly grated ginger
2 pitted prunes, chopped
stevia, to taste

Preheat the oven to 350°F (180°C/gas mark 4).

Place the apple in a small baking dish and add a little filtered water. Combine the remaining ingredients in a bowl, then press into the center of the apple.

Bake for 35–40 minutes or until cooked through. To test, pierce the apple with a sharp knife; it should slide through easily. Note: The apple can be cooked up to a day ahead, then warmed in a 350°F (180°C/gas mark 4) oven for about 20 minutes, covered with foil.

220 calories (920 kJ)

LUNCH: MUSHROOM, BROCCOLI AND SUNFLOWER SEED QUINOA PILAU
SERVES 1

1½ oz (45 g) mixed mushrooms,
    larger ones torn
½ head of broccoli, cut into florets
1 tablespoon sunflower seeds
¼ teaspoon ground cinnamon
½ teaspoon ground cumin
¼ teaspoon ground turmeric
¼ cup (¾ oz/50 g) quinoa,
    rinsed and drained
¼ cup (2 fl oz/60 ml) filtered water,
    plus extra for cooking vegetables
Himalayan salt, to taste
handful of mint, chopped (optional)

Heat a medium saucepan over medium–high heat. Add the mushrooms and broccoli with a little filtered water and cook for 5 minutes or until just softened. Add the sunflower seeds, spices and quinoa, then reduce the heat to low. Cook for 2 minutes, stirring constantly, then add the water and cook, covered, for 10–15 minutes or until the quinoa is cooked through.

Season with salt and serve topped with mint (if using).

K ▲ B ▲ P ▲ A ▲ Sw ▲ Sa ▲ So 🔘

150 calories (630 kJ)

DINNER: SPINACH AND SHRIMP CURRY
SERVES 1

Combine all the ingredients except the shrimp in a frying pan over medium heat. Bring to a boil, then reduce the heat to low and simmer for 10 minutes.

Allow to cool slightly, then transfer to a food processor and purée until smooth.

Return the mixture to the pan over low heat, then add the shrimp and cook for 5–8 minutes or until the shrimp are cooked through.

Serve immediately.

9 oz (250 g) frozen chopped spinach, thawed and drained well
1 cup (9 fl oz/250 ml) chicken stock (preferably homemade)
1 tablespoon additive-free coconut cream
2 teaspoons curry powder, or to taste
½ teaspoon ground cumin
Celtic sea salt and freshly cracked black pepper, to taste
5 raw shrimp, peeled and deveined, tails left intact

Clockwise from top left:
Baked apple with prunes,
cinnamon and cardamom;
Spinach and shrimp curry;
Mushroom, broccoli and
sunflower seed quinoa pilau

Note: Pittas should only use basmati rice and omit the salt and pepper; kaphas should halve the quantity of the ghee

KITCHARI
SERVES 4

Kitchari is nourishing, soothing and very easy to digest. Prepare a big batch and have it on hand to make a quick meal. Simply warm 1 cup of the cooked mixture with ½ cup (4 fl oz/125 ml) water and add chopped vegetables to suit your dosha (see pages 28–33). Ensure you are drinking enough water if you are doing a kitchari cleanse.

Combine all the ingredients except the salt and pepper in a large saucepan over medium heat and bring to a boil. Reduce the heat to low, then cover and simmer for 20–30 minutes or until all the water is absorbed.

Season with salt and pepper, sprinkle over extra grated turmeric (if using) and serve.

1 cup (7 oz/200 g) brown basmati or brown rice, soaked for 3 hours in filtered water and 2 tablespoons (40 ml) apple cider vinegar, then drained

1 cup (8 oz/225 g) mung beans (moong dal), soaked for 3 hours in filtered water and 2 tablespoons apple cider vinegar, then drained

1 inch (2.5 cm) piece of ginger, peeled and grated

1 inch (2.5 cm) piece of turmeric, peeled and grated, plus extra, grated, to serve (optional) *or* 2 teaspoons ground turmeric

2 teaspoons ground cumin

pinch of asafoetida

1 tablespoon ghee

4 cups (35 fl oz/1 liter) filtered water

Celtic sea salt and freshly cracked black pepper, to taste

Index

Acknowledgments

Travelling through India was one of the most eye-opening experiences of my life – it was a chaotic assault on the senses in every possible way, and without it my life would be incomplete. India altered my perception of reality forever.

During my travels, I met a myriad of wonderfully genuine and generous people who I felt had a strong sense of kinship and community. I was able to witness people's dependency on one another – but not the kind of dependency that involves getting a step ahead in business or personal advancement. What I saw was more a matter of people sticking together for the sole purpose of survival.

Being immersed in the human element of India and its people gave me an insight and a sense of perspective that can't be found on a social media highlight reel. I learned that it's not about living your dream. It's about living your purpose, and for me these two things are very different. For some people, living your purpose may be enjoying a simple, happy and uncomplicated life engulfed in personal meaning. For others it may mean the difference between a job and a calling. For me it is both.

The external chaos of India compelled me to explore my internal universe, let go of the extrinsic world and live in the intrinsic one. It helped me to cope with all that was happening externally – the people with leprosy, the snake charmers, a herd of cows on the road, bustling and beeping traffic, and a lack of sanitation.

India made me want to understand not just who I am and what my values are, but what my true purpose on this planet is. For me, being in India meant being comfortable with feeling uncomfortable most of the time, which helped me find my purpose sooner – that purpose is now sitting comfortably in your hands.

I'm so honored to have been able to write this book, which is based on my Indian food safari and my craving to delve into the richness and healing properties of Ayurvedic nutrition and cooking. I have sunk knee-deep in discovering an Ayurvedic way of life and how eating right for your constitution or dosha can bring your whole body and mind back into balance. I really hope you love this book just as much as I enjoyed writing it.

I'd like to extend my heartfelt thanks and gratitude to all of the hardworking and dedicated people who helped to bring this book into your hands.

About the Author

My publishers Murdoch Books and the wonderful Diana Hill, who is a constant source of inspiration and guidance. Christine Farmer for filling up my emotional bank account, being a pleasure to work with and re-energizing my potential for learning. My inspiring publishing team: Hugh Ford, Virginia Birch, Nicola Young, Matt Hoy, Robert Gorman, Sue Hines and Patrizia Di Biase-Dyson.

Thank you to the photographic and production team, who are an inspiring creative force: food superstar Grace Campbell, eagle-eye photographer Steve Brown, stylish stylist Sarah O'Brien and make-up artist Ilana Tischmann. Thanks also to Camilla for the beautiful clothing.

Special thanks to my travelling companion, Erica Luiz, and my friends, colleagues and mentors Louise Cornege, Kim Cotton, Juliet Potter, Howard Porter, Georgie Bridge, Rosana Lauria, Kristy Plumridge, Hilary Davis, Cindy Luken, Jessica Lowe, Pia Larsen, Kirsten Shanks, Ema Taylor, Grahame Grassby, Mike Conway and Cindy Sciberras.

All the love in the world to my family: Roxy, Arizona, Carol, Lorraine, Clive, Alex and Ben; my beautiful and very talented daughter, Tamsin Holmes, who is a huge inspiration to me; and my partner Justin – you are the love of my life and I am blessed to be able to spend every day with you.

Yours affectionately

Lee xo

Lee Holmes holds an Advanced Certificate in Food and Nutrition and is a certified holistic health coach (IIN), yoga teacher, wholefoods chef and bestselling author of the *Supercharged Food* series, which includes *Eat Your Way To Good Health*; *Eat Yourself Beautiful*; *Eat Clean, Green and Vegetarian*; *Heal Your Gut*; and *Supercharged Food For Kids*. She is a columnist for *Wellbeing Magazine* and Lifestyle Food Channel's Healthy Eating Expert, and her articles have appeared in leading Australian newspapers and journals, as well as *The Times* and *The Daily Express* in the UK and *The Huffington Post* in the US. Find Lee at her award-winning blog, superchargedfood.com.

Socialize with me

superchargedfood.com/blog
superchargedfood.com
facebook.com/superchargedfood
twitter.com/LeeSupercharged
instagram.com/leesupercharged
linkedin.com/in/leesupercharged
youtube.com/leeholmes67

Quarto is the authority on a wide range of topics.

Quarto educates, entertains and enriches the lives of our readers—enthusiasts and lovers of hands-on living.

www.QuartoKnows.com

First published in the United States of America in 2017 by Fair Winds Press, an imprint of
Quarto Publishing Group USA Inc.
100 Cummings Center
Suite 406-L
Beverly, Massachusetts 01915-6101
Telephone: (978) 282-9590
Fax: (978) 283-2742
QuartoKnows.com
Visit our blogs at QuartoKnows.com

A cataloguing-in-publication entry is available from the catalogue of the National Library of Australia at nla.gov.au.

ISBN: 978-1-59233-768-2

A catalogue record for this book is available from the British Library.

Publisher: Diana Hill
Editorial Manager: Virginia Birch
Design Manager: Hugh Ford
Design: Hugh Ford & Arielle Gamble
Editor: Nicola Young
Photographer: Steve Brown
Stylist: Sarah O'Brien
Food Editor/Home Economist: Grace Campbell
Production Manager: Mary Bjelobrk/Alex Gonzalez

Color reproduction by Splitting Image Colour Studio Pty Ltd, Clayton, Victoria
Printed by Hang Tai Printing Company Limited, China

IMPORTANT: Those who might be at risk from the effects of salmonella poisoning (the elderly, pregnant women, young children and those suffering from immune deficiency diseases) should consult their doctor with any concerns about eating raw eggs.

OVEN GUIDE: You may find cooking times vary depending on the oven you are using. For fan-forced ovens, as a general rule, set the oven temperature to 20°C (35°F) lower than indicated in the recipe.

MEASURES GUIDE: We have used 20 ml (4 teaspoon) tablespoon measures. If you are using a 15 ml (3 teaspoon) tablespoon add an extra teaspoon of the ingredient for each tablespoon specified.